ROOTS FOR RADICALS

ROOTS

FOR

RADICALS

Organizing for Power,
Action, and Justice

Edward T. Chambers

with Michael A. Cowan

continuum
NEW YORK • LONDON

The Continuum International Publishing Group Inc
15 East 26th Street, New York, NY 10010

The Continuum International Publishing Group Ltd.
The Tower Building, 11 York Road, London SE1 7NX

Printed in the United States of America

Library of Congress Cataloging-in-Publication Data

Chambers, Edward T.
Roots for radicals / Edward T. Chambers with Michael A. Cowan.
p.   cm.
Includes bibliographical references.
ISBN 0-8264-1499-0 (hardcover : alk. paper)
1. Community development—United States.   2. Community
organization—United States.   3. Community power—United States.   4.
Communication in community development—United States.   5. Group
relations training—United States.   6. Industrial Areas Foundation.
Cowan, Michael A.   II. Title.
HN90.C6C455   2003
307.1'4'0973—dc21   2003005664

To Ann and our children
Eve, Mary, Joe, Lily, and Will

"Power is actualized only where word and deed have not parted company, where words are not empty and deeds not brutal, where words are not used to veil intentions but to disclose realities, and deeds are not used to violate and destroy but to establish relations and create new realities."

Hannah Arendt
The Human Condition

"Never, never do for others what they can do for themselves."

IAF's "Iron Rule"

Contents

Foreword

Big Ed Chambers is a natural as the successor of Saul Alinsky. He was Saul's biggest disciple in more ways than one. It follows that this book, *Roots for Radicals*, completes the trilogy that Alinsky began with *Reveille for Radicals* and *Rules for Radicals*.

Big Ed picks up where Saul, in his untimely death, left off. Much has happened since 1972: three steps forward and two steps back. Cynics may say that's too sanguine an outlook, that it's the other way around, what with the few having more power than ever and the many being more powerless. Not quite so, says Chambers. Voices are heard today that were dead silent yesterday. There is, of course, a long, long way to go before the have-nots, the voiceless, find their full-throated voice.

The fact is, as Big Ed cites in chapter and verse, in one revelatory conflict after another, those voices are being heard in a surprising number of quarters, hitherto silent. There have been a surprising number of triumphs as well as defeats that need not have been.

Here is a how-to book in the best sense: a primer on how to beat the dragons. It has been designed for community organizers: to know, to feel, and mostly *to think creatively* about how to not so much lead as to *incite* the powerless to find the power and to speak themselves. It calls for social knowledge, born out of experience—with its trials and errors, and a few here-and-there knocks and blows—rather than romantic idealism.

It is not accidental that Chambers quotes the words of Nobel laureate Bernard Crick: "The more one realistically construes self-interest, the more one is involved in relationships with others . . . the more conflicts of interest or of character and circumstances will arise." Crick might have included the word "community," though that may be inferred.

Chambers is at his top form in referring to the "ABCs" of organizing. "It's not the power you possess, but using the power of the opposition against itself that changes things. It's called political *jujitsu* [an Alinsky phrase]. You must go outside the opponent's [Big Boys] experience. You aim the action for the inevitable reaction, knowing that the reaction is more important than your action itself." (I might amend Big Ed's observation: It's your action that brought the reaction about.) He recounts a victory during a black have-nots battle against Kodak's discriminatory policies in Rochester: "Organized people took on organized money and won."

One of the most moving sequences in this book deals with his beginnings as a Midwestern rural kid, being trained for the Catholic priesthood. From early on, he asked questions that were considered impudent and, indeed, sacrilegious: questions and doubts that are part of today's daily discourse and contretemps. Basically, he wanted God brought closer to the people of the parish.

That's what this book is really about. Big Ed Chambers is something of a secular priest, with the community as his parish, teaching that the least of us have the right to lead decent lives. I should point out that his first real teacher was Dorothy Day.

Studs Terkel
Chicago, Illinois

The Industrial Areas Foundation:
Social Knowledge, Power, and Politicalness

This book is about roots—roots for radicals. The late Monsignor Jack Egan of Chicago, an old friend and comrade in the struggle, suggested the title, and it fits. But "radical" is a misunderstood word for many folks today, so I need to make it clear from the start. The people you'll meet in these pages don't dress in black, wear masks, or kick in shop windows. "Radical" is from a Latin word that means "root." Radical means going to the roots of the matter, and the roots of the spirit. A radical is a person who searches for meaning and affirms community. For me, that has meant half a century of organizing for power on behalf of justice and democracy. People's public lives are fueled by a tension that won't go away, and the most radical thing they do out of that tension starts with what I call the relational meeting. More on that tension and those meetings later.

Don't expect a quick read here. These pages require that you bend back and reflect on your own life. Readers who hunger for meaning, for making sense of daily reality, should be fed here. People looking for a quick fix for what ails America, the faint of heart, and those without passion should stop now. So let's whet our appetite and go on a journey.

A little historical perspective never hurts. Nearly fifty years have passed since poverty and urban decay became matters of major attention and contention in America (eliminating slums, LBJ's war on poverty, etc.). But after decades of ideological argument and top-down bureaucratic experimentation, our cities are still drowning in poor people, violence, and desperation. During that same period, our public life has been eroded by the isolation and anxiety of consumerism, unfettered capitalism, and social divisions. The capacity of everyday ordinary people to make room at the table of public life for folk from other cultures is strained. The problems of the cities, the economic pressures of the market, and the increasing diversity of cultures aren't going away. We have senators for oil and gas, and senators for farmers, but none for cities or families. Democratic self-governance—public conversation and collaborative action by organized citizens—remains our best hope for dealing with these challenges. That's the radical message of this book.

In the world as it should be, democracy means participation in public decisions in which all are included because of the dignity of being "created equal." In the real world, democracy is dominated by the interests of a few wealthy and powerful institutions. A truly democratic public life requires the organization, education, and development of leaders who regard themselves as equal, sovereign citizens with the know-how to stand for the whole. We're not born with these civic skills and virtues, and today's instant gratification culture constantly undermines them. The radical question of this book is, why should things be this way, rather than another?

Since its founding by Saul Alinsky in 1940, the Industrial Areas Foundation (hereafter, IAF), meaning "Urban Areas Foundation," has worked with citizens, both people of faith and seculars, to build broad organizations that don't rely on liberal belief in the welfare state or conservative faith in the invisible hand of the market.[1] Instead, the IAF has invested in the power of organized families and congregations acting together to refound democratic public life. By staying on this course, the IAF has been instrumental in the creation of more than sixty independent, nonpartisan, dues-based citizens organizations throughout the United States and has encouraged the development of such organizations in the United Kingdom, Germany, and South Africa. By winning on issues in places where both state and market have failed, our broad-based citizens organizations lead the way in showing how civil-society institutions can be a source of powerful citizen participation and a creative way to achieve social change. The radical question of this book is, why not a different world?

In the Back of the Yards and TWO organizations in Chicago and the FIGHT organization in Rochester, New York, foundational and universal insights about organizing people were discovered and crafted. In San Antonio, a city where people of one culture formerly functioned as menial laborers for those of another, a vibrant, bicultural political community has been achieved. In East London, civic participation has emerged within a mix of cultures and religions that those radical predecessors of ours who founded the mother of parliaments could never have imagined on English soil. In New York, large communities of new working-class homeowners reside where politicians and experts said they never would. In Baltimore, a comprehensive scholarship and jobs incentive program for public high school graduates and a co-op of temporary workers have been created. In the cities and suburbs of Chicago and Boston, the foundation has been laid for metropolitan-wide, culturally diverse, broad-based citizens organizations on a size and scale never before attempted, one appropriate to the complexities of the twenty-first century.

Two defining characteristics of IAF organizations are their plurality and inclusiveness. Within our organizations, citizens whose ancestors were born in the United States, Europe, Africa, Latin America, Asia, the Middle East, and North America collaborate as equal partners in the pursuit of justice and opportunity for all faiths, cultures, and classes. Within our organizations, Jews, Christians, Muslims, Hindus, and Buddhists join together to seek the well-being of their cities. (Rumor has it that a few New Age types have been spotted recently.) Within our organizations, women and men share leadership, authority, and public roles. Within our organizations, city dwellers, suburbanites, and rural residents come together to face issues that none can address alone. Within our organizations, people who believe in God, democracy, or both pursue matters of mutual interest. Within our organizations, some political conservatives, lots of moderates, and some liberals seek common ground, refusing to allow ideological differences to perpetuate social divisions. Members of IAF organizations understand that while the "silent majority" goes along with the status quo, it only takes a well-organized 2 to 3 percent of the body politic to initiate social change. That's the radical message of this book.

Readers familiar with the reputation of our organizations for dramatic, imaginative and effective public action may be surprised to find that the first—and most critical—chapter waiting for you here is an extended reflection on the tension between concrete realities and cherished ideals. Such a response, however, betrays a simplistic grasp of organizing in the IAF tradition. The liturgy of public life developed by our professional organizers and citizen leaders over the course of sixty years of organizing, teaching, and mentoring ordinary people in the practice of citizenship is "research, action, evaluation." Action is the middle term in a three-part formula, sandwiched between moments of hard reflection. The intentional discipline of IAF organizing requires that public actions begin and end in reflection. While no one develops a public life without action, we only learn how to build the power to act for justice in the real world when public actions are preceded and followed by disciplined reflection.

The time has come for me to put into words something of the formidable practical know-how about doing nonpartisan politics that has been gleaned from thousands of public actions, hours of disciplined reflection, and a two-generation effort in education for grassroots public leadership by the IAF. That body of social knowledge is the root of this book.

Social Knowledge and Politics

The Greek word for knowledge most familiar to us is *theoria*, or theory. That's the knowledge that comes from the reasoning and research of academics. You get it by pulling away from the realities of everyday life into a university or laboratory, a specialized place of research, ideas, and academic jargon. Those of us on the outside usually call it the ivory tower. But there is another Greek word for knowledge, *phronesis*, which means "practical wisdom." That's the kind of know-how based on the hard lessons of life experience that guide a good parent, boss, or leader. It's what I call social knowledge. People gain social knowledge by dealing with others around life's everyday demands. It comes from the actual experience of raising children, running businesses, and dealing with conflicts. It's learned on the street, in private relationships, and in public places. You earn it only by digesting your own life experiences and those of others. All social knowledge is experiential: You don't get it in school; you get it at work, on the streets, and at home.

Andres Sarabia is one of the most experienced leaders in the IAF network. He has been with San Antonio's Communities Organized for Public Service (COPS) organization since 1974, serving as its first president from 1974 to 1976.

He recalls a critical meeting from the early days of COPS, when hundreds of members of the new organization gathered in the auditorium of a local school to confront public officials and force them to solve the severe flooding problems that resulted from the lack of proper drainage and sewers in poor neighborhoods. As film of submerged cars, houses, and entire streets was shown to the audience, people became more and more angry. Emotions were running so high that there was potential for trouble.

But Sarabia and the other leaders of COPS had been trained. They had been briefed on every potential problem, and they had determined in advance what response they would have. "Much to the surprise of the city officials, we had total control of the assembly, and we were able to direct the anger of the people into a positive and productive meeting," says Sarabia.

He is convinced that this kind of training and discipline is what has positioned COPS among the most powerful broad-based organizations in the country. It has also given him the confidence and ability to handle difficult situations in all areas of his life. His years as a leader in COPS have taught him how to channel and focus his own anger regarding injustice, so that instead of useless or even dangerous action, he could actually alter the way the system works in San Antonio and effect changes in the way people are treated.

He also uses his leadership skills at work, where he is a computer specialist in the civil service. He uses what he has learned about reflection and planning, confrontation, and negotiation to effect an increase in the number of Hispanics who are promoted in his section. His training and experience as an organizational leader have also had an impact in his personal life.

He once wrote to his son, who was a U.S. Marine preparing to be shipped overseas for combat. Sarabia explained to him the difference between channeled and uncontrolled anger, and the importance of reflection before confrontation and action, about making sure that he had his fellow soldiers with him before he made any moves.

"Survival skills," Sarabia calls them.

People with this kind of practical know-how earned it in moments of challenge and struggle, on the street—not in the ivory tower. They are the shrewd women and men of Matthew's Sermon on the Mount who build their houses on rock, so that they remain standing through life's inevitable storms. Others naturally recognize this real-life wisdom grounded in experience and turn to those who demonstrate it for guidance and leadership in facing the urgent questions of everyday life.

This book is in the genre of social, not theoretical, knowledge. Its roots are in the body of social knowledge about politics that has been acquired and refined collectively by the organizers and leaders of the IAF over more than fifty years, men and women like Andres Sarabia, and others whose stories await you in these pages. When I say "politics" I don't mean the corrupt, money-driven, partisan electoral activity that usually goes by that name; I'm returning to the ancient meaning of politics as adults coming together in public places as sovereign citizens to deliberate and act for the common good. Bill Greider catches the meaning of politics in the following passage from his agitational book on the state of American democracy.

> Politics is not a game. It exists to resolve the largest questions of the society—the agreed-upon terms by which everyone can live peaceably with one another. At its best politics creates and sustains social relation-

ships—the human conversation and engagement that draw people together and allow them to discover their mutuality.[2]

In the collective social knowledge and shared vision of the professional organizers and citizen leaders of the IAF network, there resides a precious storehouse of practical know-how about public life. These men and women understand what it means in practice to make common cause with people of other races, religions, and neighborhoods in seeking the good of larger civic communities. They have experienced victories and endured defeats in the public arena, and they have done both in the company of former strangers now become fellow citizens. That's the root message of this book.

Because electoral politics has been so degraded since World War II, I will often use the clarifying word "politicalness" in these pages, to reclaim Aristotle's definition of politics as the capacity to gather with others as fellow citizens to converse, plan, act, and reflect for the well-being of people as a whole.[3] Radically speaking, our politicalness is an inheritance bestowed by the Creator through our parents. It's our birthright. We receive the gifts "to be able" (called power) coupled with "to be related in a bond of affinity with others" (called love). Like our sexuality, politicalness is given to us at birth. Sexuality and politicalness relate us to one another in reciprocal bonds of affinity and accountability. That neither of these powers can be realized in isolation makes it plain that humans are interdependent, relational beings. Because sexuality (our passions, all of them) and politicalness (drives, self-interest, élan) are primary sources of the vitality that animates human life, failing to develop these dimensions of personhood means severe limitations on the meaning, joy, and creativity we can experience in life. Developing the birthrights the Creator gave us of politicalness and sexuality requires and nurtures deep forms of social knowledge. The concept of "citizen" is based in the nation; the concept of "person" is universal, because it is based on our birthright of sexuality and politicalness. They can take away your citizenship, but not your personhood. That's the radical message of this book.

During the last sixty years of IAF training and mentoring, our leaders and organizers have developed their politicalness by researching, acting, and reflecting for themselves and for the common good in cities, suburbs, and rural areas across the United States and on other continents. Prior to the writing of this book, this evolving social knowledge drawn from real-life IAF organizing has been taught in local and national training sessions by experienced organizers and leaders who gained their social knowledge of political action by engagement and reflection in local organizations. The purpose of this book is to distill the basic elements of the IAF's hard-won practical wisdom from our oral tradition into written form so that people and institutions seeking to change themselves into effective actors for the common good can draw on it.

So let's start. In the first chapter I lay out the paradigm of The Two Worlds, which has been patiently crafted and taught in the crucible of public action and reflection by IAF organizations over the past thirty years. It's the foundation on which all effective organizing rests, *the* root for radicals.

1

The World As It Is
and the World As It Should Be

"Out of such crooked timbers as man is made, nothing entirely
straight can be fashioned."

IMMANUEL KANT

The Two Worlds

Until we die, we live with a tension under our skin at the center of our
personhood. We are born into a world of needs and necessities, opportunities
and limitations, and must survive there. No one has the luxury of ignoring
these realities. Self-preservation, food, clothing, shelter, safety, health care,
education, and work are necessary for everyone. Large numbers of people
agonize over these things every day of their lives; many of us think of nothing
else. This demanding set of real circumstances, which we didn't create but
which we are thrown into, is the world as it is. When people refer to the "real
world" in conversation, this is what they mean.

We also have dreams and expectations, yearnings and values, hopes and
aspirations. We exist from day-to-day with the awareness that things not only
might, but could be, should be, different for ourselves and our children. We
know that we don't fulfill ourselves, that there is an ideal, a greater good that
matters. We are a mysterious combination of matter and spirit, body and
soul, sexuality and power. We aren't born with realized vision and values. We
inherit them from our parents, teachers, and the received culture, which is all
around us. It's like the air we breathe—we can't escape it. As we grow and
move into adulthood, these formative patterns of the good and meaningful
life must be acted upon to become real. The guiding ideals that we receive
from our culture and predecessors make up the world as it should be. Cynics
deride vision and values as irrelevant in the real world, but the fact is that
they are indispensable to our sanity, integrity, and authenticity.

"As is" and "should be"—*is* and *ought*—are abstractions. They don't exist as such. You can break them apart the way I just did, but only for the purpose of understanding. In real life, the two always exist conjugally. Just as there is no such thing as culture without society, and no such thing as person without family, so it is with the two worlds. Like the encircling polarities of the Chinese yin/yang symbol, the two worlds always function in relationship to each other. Just as good/evil, active/passive, and light/dark have no meaning if you break them in half, so it is with the two worlds. Their reality *is* their relationship, the tense, constantly shifting interplay between them. The hard existential truth is that from the awakening of our consciences until we lay down in death, we feel an unrelenting struggle between is and ought.

Let's pause for a minute. Is this two-world stuff fair? No. We are crooked timbers by nature, made of matter and spirit, and brought into being by parents nobody asked us about. We are given a short life, one of constant struggle. We are supposed to love ourselves and others. So why in God's name do we have to live in two worlds? Why aren't we born straight instead of crooked, with no in-betweens, no more-or-less? The answer is freedom—to think, to feel, to imagine, to will, and to act. There is the trade-off for being born crooked: In the midst of the tension of living in between the two worlds, our spirit is free.

Having just described the relationship between the two worlds as tense, let me be clear about what I mean by tension. In today's culture, tension is a bad word, always quickly followed in advertising by "relief." The media teaches that tensions mean we're "stressed out" or "uptight" or "wound up"—all undesirable states calling for immediate medication, therapy, or exercise. But the tension I'm naming here isn't a problem to be solved. It's the human condition. It's the gap that people who aren't completely lost in the culture of self-centeredness feel between the reality that surrounds them and their ideals. Philosophers use the word "dialectical" to name a back-and-forth tension between interrelated poles, and I will sometimes use it to describe the relationship between the two worlds.

Whenever I draw attention to one of the two worlds, I'm always conscious that its partner is present, and you should be, too. It's sunup and sundown. One makes no sense without the other. I call the world as it is and the world as it should be *conjugal* concepts. Like all relational partners, they shape and inform each other. You can't understand sexual intercourse by looking at one partner in isolation, and you can't grasp the two worlds by dividing them. The foundational conviction of the IAF organizing tradition is that it is the fate of human beings to exist *in-between* the world as it is and the world as it should be. Reflective people of conscience are constantly and painfully aware of the gap between our so-called values and the facts of life in the everyday world within which we operate. When these two worlds collide hard enough and often enough, a fire in the belly is sometimes ignited. The tension between the two worlds is the root of radical action for justice and democracy—not radical as in looting or trashing, but as in going to the root of things.

Wind, rain, and fog confronted Carol Reckling, a senior leader in Baltimoreans United in Leadership Development (BUILD), when she left her office and dashed toward her car on a miserable midwinter dusk in downtown Baltimore. This was the night that BUILD had chosen for an action involving 1,000 leaders with Maryland state legislators in Annapolis.

She recalled that the weather had also been miserable on that night seven years before when she began her work with BUILD. Although she had been aware of the organization since its inception, she had shied away from participating until she learned of a meeting that would focus on a matter near to her heart: schools. The meeting was a caucus of the just-forming BUILD education committee. The subject was not curriculum or funding or the condition of buildings, but something more basic—a lack of supplies. No paper. No pencils. No books. She remembered her feelings—shock, then anger—at hearing that litany. No paper. No pencils. No books. Reckling herself had received a good education in Baltimore elementary and high schools, at Howard University, and in the master's program of Washington University Business School. She had found teachers along the way who worked hard and worked her hard. And she had lived, firsthand, what her parents and their peers had always said: "Education is the key." So she understood full well the whole equation facing too many of Baltimore's children: No paper, no pencils, no books = no career, no future, no hope.

In the years since that first meeting, she had worked hard and well. She had become a driving force in education strategy in Baltimore. She had negotiated with three mayors and many corporate leaders. She had been one of the founders of BUILD's Commonwealth Strategy, which guarantees full funding for postsecondary education or initial employment opportunities to all graduates of the Baltimore public schools who meet specified attendance and performance criteria.

Carol Reckling had been taught by her parents and her church to appreciate the value of education—so much so, that when she saw large numbers of Baltimore's children being denied its basics, she was moved to act. The constant tension between the world as it is and the world as it should be is the primary motivation leading people like Carol Reckling to seek the common good. What I mean by being moral or ethical is stepping up to the tension between the two worlds. As I hope to make plain in the final section of this chapter, understanding the world as it is while ignoring the world as it should be leads to cynicism, division, and coercion. Concern for the world as it should be divorced from the capacity for analysis and action in the world as it is marginalizes and sentimentalizes morality and ethics. IAF's position is that maintaining a good enough tension between the two worlds is the hallmark of authentically moral and ethical human living. Embracing this tension every day is our spiritual destiny.

In a world conscious of cultural diversity, I need to add a nuance here. The tension between the two worlds is a tension between interpretations. The world as it is and the world as it should be are not raw facts or simple objective realities. We don't have objective, uninterpreted access to either world. People from different histories see the two worlds differently. Any group's readings of what's happening in a situation (the world as it is) and the key values in that situation (the world as it should be) are interpretations from that group's perspective. When we meet in public life, I bring my group's interpretations of the world as it is and as it should be, and you bring your group's interpretations. What you and I can create for our respective groups or institutions and the larger community depends on bringing our respective interpretations together in a better reading of our common situation and obligations than we could do alone, one that enables us to act together with power despite our differences.

Uneasiness in the face of the disparity between the two worlds haunts us throughout our lives. It isn't a problem that can be fixed, or a temporary state of affairs that we can end by getting things right. It's the human condition. It's possible to reduce the tension between the two worlds through consumption, addiction, or just giving in to the frenetic pace of modern life. We can and do numb ourselves to the gap between the social reality we encounter and our best hopes and aspirations. When this numbness sets in, our humanity is diminished; when it takes over, our humanity is lost.

Living In-Between the Two Worlds

It is useful to break down the relationship between the two worlds into four polarities, each of which contributes to the overall tension. The four are represented in the following diagram, which is an abstraction.

Polarities Between the Two Worlds

The World As It Is ⟵ *tension* ⟶ *The World As It Should Be*

Self-Interest ⟷ Self-Sacrifice
Power ⟷ Love
Change ⟷ Unity
Imagination ⟷ Hope

Self-Interest ⟷ Self-Sacrifice

The first polarity between the two worlds is between self-interest and self-sacrifice. Self-interest evokes a range of responses. To realists centered on the world as it is, self-interest is obviously the prime motivator of human behavior. Pursuing self-interest is as natural as breathing. For idealists focused on the world as it should be, self-interest is another word for selfishness. It's an isolating form of individualism with little regard for others. Both of these views convey a partial truth, but miss a deeper one.

Self-interest is the natural concern of a creature for its survival and well-being. It's the fundamental priority underlying the choices we make. Self-interest is based on nature's mandate that we secure the basic needs and necessities of life, and develops further to include more complex desires and requirements. Healthy self-interest is one of the marks of integrity or wholeness in a person. It is the source of the initiative, creativity, and drive of human beings who are fully alive.

The English word "interest" is a combination of two Latin words, *inter*, meaning "between" or "among," and *esse*, meaning "to be." Our interests do not reside inside our skins but in between, within our relationships with others. Philosopher Hannah Arendt writes, ". . . the language of the Romans, perhaps the most political people we have known, used the words 'to live' and 'to be among men' (*inter homines esse*) or 'to die' and 'to cease to be among men' (*inter homines esse desinere*) as synonyms."[1] To live is to be among people, to have interests. Human beings are interpersonal beings, relational selves.

Self-preservation, self-recognition, self-determination, and self-respect are components of self-interest. Self-preservation is the drive for survival; it's so strong that we can take life to defend ourselves. Self-recognition is the ability to claim our place and space in the world whether others have acknowledged it yet or not. Self-determination is the capacity to expand and deepen our abilities through creative, self-initiated action. Self-respect is recognition of our uniqueness. Self-interest rightly understood includes all of these dimensions. The opposite of self-interest is suicide or self-destruction.

Genuine self-interest is illustrated in the following story.

For thirty years, Sister Mary Beth Larkin has been a member of a Catholic women's religious order. Although interested in religious life, she did not want to teach or work in a hospital. She thought she wanted to do social work, but seven years of experience with providing crisis intervention and direct service for the poor was so frustrating that she nearly left her community. She knew how to help people work the system, but what about getting the system to work for people?

She found a way to do just that. While working in a Los Angeles parish, she became involved in the United Neighborhoods Organization (UNO). She was deeply impressed with the power and effectiveness of the organization in getting real changes for people living in poor neighborhoods. One of her first public actions involved getting up on the stage before the city council and translating a speech for a Spanish-speaking leader. "I was so nervous that I was literally sick. I thought about calling in and saying I couldn't make it. But when the UNO leaders who were present in that hall called the meeting to order and the council members ignored us, I suddenly got very angry, angry for myself and for all those people who deserved better treatment than that. Once I got angry, I was fine. I realized that there is a public person in me that I never knew was there. It was a liberating experience."

Her commitment to religious life renewed, Sister Mary Beth knew that what she wanted was to organize people and work with them so they could get what they wanted. She knew that this was where she belonged, but no one in her order had ever been involved in anything like IAF organizing before, and there were feelings within the order that this kind of work might not be appropriate for a sister. Eventually, she was permitted to take a position as a full-time organizer and went on to organize in Queens, New York, in San Antonio, and in other parts of Texas. As an IAF organizer, she is usually unable to live with her community of sisters in California. She calls that one of the sacrifices she had to make to do the work that allows her religious convictions to have meaning.

Her work as an organizer has allowed Sister Mary Beth to stay with her commitment to religious life. She expresses her delight with this role by explaining that "religious life is public life. It's about making a difference and doing the difficult work of seeking justice in a society. It's the work of the Gospel—we must take action to achieve justice."

Self-interest defined too narrowly becomes selfishness. This occurs, for example, when self-interest is reduced to how many cars or homes you own, or how large your stock portfolio is. Whether self-interest degenerates into selfishness and meaninglessness or not depends upon how well it is held in creative tension with its conjugal partner.

Self-sacrifice is the counterpart of self-interest. If self-interest involves knowing when and how to assert your concerns effectively, self-sacrifice means being able to suppress your own interests for others.

Self-interest and self-sacrifice are forever joined in a give-and-take relationship. Jewish, Christian, Islamic, and other traditions long ago highlighted the great paradox of human existence: Giving up one's life for another is the highest good. In real life, we are always more or less concerned with self and others. Good parents, teachers, friends, and leaders understand that there are times when their well-being requires curbing or postponing action on their own behalf to take account of others' interests. They also know that there are moments when they must strongly pursue their own interests, but without unnecessary harm to others.

The first polarity between the world as it is and the world as it should be, then, is the tension between self-interest and self-sacrifice. As with each of the four polarities, there is no formula for weighing self-interest against self-sacrifice in particular situations. That balancing act requires seasoned judgment based on social knowledge, which comes only from ongoing action, reflection, and evaluation.

Power ←——→ Love

The second polarity between the two worlds is between power and love. Power is a loaded word. Those who call themselves realists take it for granted and try to use it shrewdly in pursuing their agendas. Idealists are prone to see power as negative if not downright evil, as something to be avoided. A cardinal archbishop once said to me, "I have trouble with the word 'power'; I call it truth." He didn't understand that power has a Trinitarian character: I and you create a "we the people," a new reality. Beyond minimal forms like voting or jury duty, ordinary people have little direct experience of exercising power in public life.

Power is the ability to act. Like the capacity to love, it is given to us at birth. Power is our birthright, our inheritance. It is the basis of our capacity to address differences through politics. From one perspective, power is neutral. It may be used for evil or for good. From another, it is ambiguous because any employment of power by finite human beings, no matter how well intended and successful, will lead to unexpected consequences for self and others. Hannah Arendt was correct in observing that one of the defining characteristics of all human action is the unpredictability of its effects.

In Western culture, power has come to be interpreted and practiced as one-way influence. According to this understanding, one person's power is his or her ability to get someone else to do what he or she wants; the other person's power is the ability to do as that person chooses. In a power encounter, it's one against the other. Whoever ends up making the other move more has demonstrated more power. Here, power means "power over."

Because they have no verb "to power," English speakers have a harder time understanding that power is more like a verb than a noun than do Spanish speakers, who routinely use the verb *poder,* meaning "to be able," "to have the capacity to have an influence," "to power." English speakers not only misunderstand power as a noun, as something that can be possessed and used at will as an instrument, but also assume that it exists in a fixed quantity. Just as there is only so much gold in the world, there is only so much power to go around. If I get some more, you lose it. This is power understood as unilateral and as limited in quantity. But power is not zero-sum.

Power has another face that the unilateral definition prevents us from seeing plainly. Even in its most crass, dominating form, power takes place in relationships. Think about it. Does the concept of power make sense without another to receive our influence? Seeing clearly that every act of power requires a relationship is the first step toward realizing that the capacity to be affected by another is the other side of the coin named power. If you are finding this concept difficult to grasp, it is probably because the unilateral definition of power is so ingrained in you by schooling, the media culture, and pundits.

People who can understand the concerns of others and mix those concerns with their own agenda have access to a power source denied to those who can push only their own interests. In this fuller understanding, "power" is a verb meaning "to give and take," "to be reciprocal," "to be influenced as well to influence." To be affected by another in relationship is as true a sign of power as the capacity to affect others. Relational power is infinite and unifying, not limited and divisive. It's additive and multiplicative, not subtractive and divisive. As you become more powerful, so do those in relationship with you. As they become more powerful, so do you. This is power understood as relational, as power *with,* not *over.*[2]

In January of 1978 New York City's newly elected mayor Ed Koch fulfilled a promise he had made to the leaders of a new and growing force in Queens politics—Queens Citizens Organization (QCO). During his campaign, Koch had pledged that if he were elected mayor, one of his first acts would be to come to a public meeting of QCO leaders.

At 8:00 P.M., 1,500 leaders were seated and ready at St. Thomas the Apostle auditorium. Mayor Koch was led in by a procession of local school children and followed by an army of TV cameras. As soon as the mayor had taken his seat on the dais, Father Eugene Lynch, co-chair of QCO, took the podium to begin the meeting.

The mayor had other ideas. Rising from his seat, he announced that he had a speech he wanted to give before the meeting went any farther. Father Lynch replied that there was a full agenda of QCO issues and ideas that were scheduled to be addressed, and that Koch would be given a chance to speak near the end of the meeting. The mayor countered that if he were not granted ten minutes to speak immediately, he would walk out.

Father Lynch and the QCO strategy team were confused. They called time-out, caucused, and decided to grant Koch two minutes to speak. Father Lynch announced their decision, but Koch replied that that wasn't good enough. To the boos and hisses of the crowd gathered there, he walked out. As he proceeded out the door, he turned to the pursuing press corps and snarled, "These people don't seem to understand. The election is over!"

It soon became apparent that what at first seemed a terrible blow to QCO would actually turn into a great victory. That evening on the eleven o'clock news and the next morning in *The New York Times* and *The Daily News,* reporters depicted an arrogant politician thumbing his nose at hard-working Queens families. Such words as "emperor" and "arrogant" laced the headlines describing Koch's behavior. Finally, the mayor capitulated, inviting QCO leaders to City Hall to reconcile. With its first major victory, QCO exploded into the New York City political arena with unprecedented fanfare.

This story shows both unilateral and relational power in action. Threatening to leave if you can't have your way and storming out when you don't get it are unilateral-power moves. Attempting to negotiate a compromise on the spot and accepting the offer to reconcile when the time is right are relational-power moves. Unilateral power is interested only in the pursuit of its own agenda. Relational power includes others' interests in its agenda. And sometimes relational power wins. When ordinary people get organized, they can hold powerful public officials—like the mayor of New York City—

accountable. When ordinary people get organized, they become citizens with some power.

Like self-interest, power can realize itself fully only if held in creative relationship with its conjugal partner, which is love. Love is a loaded term. Realists see no place for love in what they call the real world, especially the world beyond family and friendship. Idealists regard love as the ultimate reality, as a force actively working to bring justice and mercy to the world.

People usually take it for granted that the crux of love is focusing on the other, while downplaying or sacrificing one's self. If exercising power means asserting one's self-interest, loving means disregarding it. Love is treated as the opposite of power. This is love understood as unilateral.

But there is a truer dimension to love that a unilateral perspective hides. The mandate from the Hebrew scriptures to love one's neighbor as one's self does not imply ignoring one's self-interest. To love the neighbor *as* the self is to respect the neighbor's interests and one's own equally. In a similar vein, the basic ethical principle in Western philosophy—the famous "categorical imperative" of the same Kant who brought us the crooked timbers—is that one should never treat a human being only as a means to some end. The relational nature of interests comes into play here. Love means sustaining relationships in which the interdependence of one's own and others' interests is recognized and respected. This is love understood as a mutual, reciprocal process of give and take.

The received culture wants to privatize love, but love is not limited to the private sphere. Love occurs in public relationships when people come together despite their differences to thrash out issues affecting the well-being of their community, not splintering into narrow factions, but holding their differing interests in respectful, creative tension. IAF leaders, like the collective that publicly confronted Mayor Koch in the story you just read, are committed to and practiced in the arts of public discussion, shared action, reasonable compromise, and joint reflection.

Social knowledge drawn from the IAF's experience over the past sixty years in assisting ordinary citizens to organize for power to bring about change in their communities is the source of my judgment that the realist and idealist interpretations of power and love are distortions. In Western culture, "power" means "unilateral power" and "love" means "unilateral love." So it should be no surprise that Westerners tend to see power and love as opposites, and the right relationship between them as a kind of balancing off of the effects of these two ways of relating. When we "power" someone, we ignore their interests; when we "love" someone, we ignore our own concerns. If you happen to hold these conceptions of power and love, you are profoundly mistaken, but you are not alone.

Power and love—like self-interest and self-sacrifice—are not mutually exclusive but rather complementary aspects of a conjugal partnership. There can be no creative power without some acknowledgment of the other's interests, just as there can be no healthy love if the self is wholly lost in concern for the other. The love that lays down its life for another is a paradoxical yet coherent act of self-respect. As any good parent, police officer, or team player knows, there are many moments when one's own comfort or convenience or preference is not one's most pressing concern.

The second polarity between the world as it is and the world as it should be, then, is the tension between power and love. Reinhold Niebuhr had it right: "Power without love is tyranny, and love without power is sentimentality." In power and love, the interests of both parties matter. To power and love well is to respect the other and the self. In relational power, effects are given and received. Understanding the relational character of power and love transforms the practice of both because both require give-and-take relationships. Power and love are two-way streets.

Change ⟷ Unity

The third polarity between the world as it is and the world as it should be is between change and unity. The ancient Greek philosopher Heraclitus said, "It is necessary to know that . . . justice is conflict, that all things come about in conflict and in accordance with necessity." More than 2,000 years later, his keen grasp of the realities of power led IAF founder Saul Alinsky to state the following *law of change*: "Change means movement; movement means friction; friction means heat; heat means controversy." Just as in the physics of the material world, so in the realm of "social physics" there is no change without the movement of action, no movement without the friction of competing interests, and no friction without the heat of controversy. There is no nice, polite way to get change.

What led Alinsky to this conclusion? The pursuit of interests always plays out between and among people. The status quo in any particular set of circumstances in the world as it is always gives some groups advantages over others. Initiatives for change will be perceived as threats by those with vested interest, and thus as controversial. "Power," as former slave turned abolitionist Frederick Douglass rightly insisted, "concedes nothing voluntarily." There is no change without the friction of interests in confrontation.

In the dynamics of social change, differing interests will surface whenever people organize to change the status quo. Facing these differences and dealing with them straightforwardly requires that we exercise our ability to negotiate. History teaches plainly that conflicts of interest that are not resolvable through political means will be settled by one or another form of unilateral power, usually violence. All authentic politics deals with differences through constructive compromises, without force or violence.

Unity, a state of harmony or peace, is the counterpart of change. We have a need deep inside of us that cries out for peace and quiet. A mother raising three small children; the executive caught between the boss and customers, trying to please both parties, and pleasing neither; the person with dark skin snubbed with a remark like "the trouble with you people is. . . ."; the sixty-five-year-old priest whose archbishop tells him that he is "too pastoral" and eases him out after years of ministry; the parents whose sixteen-year-old son borrows Dad's car for some fun after school with his buddy and proceeds to roll it, breaking his teeth, face, and collar bones, and nearly bleeding to death—all want a world of fairness and repose.

Conflict, friction, and confrontation are what the world as it is serves up. Is it fair? No, but it is the price of free will. We are not made straight but crooked, caught between constant change and our wish for harmony. Fleeting moments of peace and harmony are the most we get in this life. The holy books promise lasting peace, but only when the reign of God arrives. Until then, unity in the real world lasts for thirty seconds or maybe a day and a half. The law of change is incessant, like the tides. The yearning for unity is like the longing for certainty. We want both, but we can't have them in this lifetime.

Do you think radical organizers and leaders like conflict? No! Some kamikaze movement types do; they live for so-called action. They don't understand that all action is in the inevitable reaction. What counts is not what you do; it's what they do in response to what you do that matters. A creative tension between change and harmony is exemplified by broad-based citizens organizations, like this one in the IAF network.

One thousand black and white Memphians spilled out of the Golden Leaf Baptist Church in North Memphis to kick off the organizing drive in Memphis and Shelby County by Shelby County Interfaith (SCI). Representatives of thirty-five congregations, along with the bishops of the Episcopal and Roman Catholic dioceses and the national president of the Progressive Baptist Convention, had come to commit themselves to the most important organizing effort in Memphis since the civil rights movement. Most significant for this racially polarized Southern city, half the congregations were black and half were white. They represented nearly every neighborhood of Memphis: the wealthy, the middle class, the working class, and the poor. Those who attended called the new organization the most significant black and white effort in the city's history.

The central message of the worship service was contained in the question that Dr. Alan V. Ragland of the New Fellowship Baptist Church put to the crowd: "Are you ready to work together?" He then challenged those present more pointedly: "Are you white members here tonight ready to hold black hands, even when they want to pull away?" "Yes!" came the response to resounding applause. Then: "Are you black members here tonight ready to hold white hands, even when they want to pull away?" Again, the answer was a powerful "Yes!" accompanied by applause from the entire assembly.

When the worship service ended, black and white Memphians went out to begin a new experiment in democracy in the heart of the Old South. In the city where Dr. Martin Luther King's life had been taken in an act of racial hatred, his dream of an America where character, not skin color, would be the measure of a person's worth lived on.

We yearn for the peace of unity, for moments like the one just described in Memphis, in which blacks and whites joined together to stand for the good of the whole city. The law of change, however, complicates this yearning, since there is no change without friction. How can we reconcile the law of change with our desire for oneness? The unavoidable struggle and friction required for any real change must be understood as a necessary part of the resolution of tensions arising from conflicting insights. In real life, people coming from different histories, like Latinos and Anglos, blacks and whites, new immigrants and established residents in the United States, see the two worlds differently. Strong public relationships require acknowledging differences.

The deeply felt wish for harmony constantly tempts people, especially idealists, to avoid the necessary friction that comes when real differences are faced. Let's be honest. I rarely wake up saying, "God, I hope this will be a controversial, friction-filled day." Do you? But so-called harmony based on avoiding what really divides us is falsely named. In reality, such a limited form of public relationship is a misguided denial of a real building block—our different viewpoints. It prevents the tough talk that leads to half or three quarters of a loaf.

"Civility" and "citizen" come from the same Latin word. Treating someone civilly doesn't mean being polite; it means treating her or him as a fellow citizen, as someone whose uniqueness must be respected and included, some-one with whom one must converse, debate, seek compromise, and collabo-rate. In public life, politeness is not civility; it's the sin of the middle class yearning to join the ranks of the haves. It is the refuge of those who have not developed their political capacity to the point where they can stand the ten-sion and heat of controversy. The law of change demands that we don't just huddle with our own group, but risk bringing real differences to the common table for resolution. In creating the public actions that the law of change demands, a process unfolds in which we grow in our capacity to be public people, that is, in our ability to stand for the whole.

Maintaining creative tension between change and unity requires that we move beyond isolated politeness into collective public actions that include both the acknowledgment of real differences and the search for workable compromises. The common good of a large and diverse community can be pursued effectively only when a representative collective of institutions is bold enough to stand for the whole. It can be advanced only when real differences are bound up together in a web of relationships anchored in the institutions that bring citizens and people of faith together—churches, neighborhood groups, labor unions, and other associations. Public relationships both re-quire and bring forth the ability to live with the inevitable tensions of com-mon life. A politics anchored in such bonds must be able to bear the necessary uneasiness between the law of change and harmony.

Imagination ←——→ Hope

The final polarity between the two worlds is between imagination and hope. Imagination is connected to memory. What we remember makes possible and limits how we understand the signs of our time; how we understand those signs makes possible and limits the future we can imagine. Imagination and memory allow us to recall, reflect, relive, and reorganize.

Imagination is a gift, a unique faculty like good instinct, but it frequently gets lost in our modern worship of intellect and will. Imagination is no less important than our abilities to think and choose. Imagination lets us glimpse a world that has not yet materialized and move mentally back and forth be-tween what was and what is, and what is and what might be. Although dis-missed as mere fantasy since the Enlightenment, which sanctified reason and will, imagination is what allows the tension of living between the two worlds to create newness, first in our mind and body, and then, through our actions, in reality. The Russian philosopher Nikolay Berdyayev said, "The faculty of imagination is the source of all creativeness. . . . Without it there can be no works of art, no scientific or technical discoveries, no plan for ordering the economic or the political life of nations."[3]

Since Freud, people in the West have been frightened by instinct. But the so-called sixth sense should be honored as a faculty along with intellect and will. My experience convinces me that most people have good instincts but don't trust them. Your instincts are like your intuition and passion—the key to all creative activity. Imagination is grounded in the body, where the human spirit resides and the instrument through which it acts. Everyday, ordinary people figure out how to feed and clothe themselves, make a living, have sex, raise children, and solve problems through the development of their instinctual social know-how.

The saint of the imaginative faculty is Einstein. His thought experiments, which took place in his own imagination, utterly changed the world for better and for worse. He understood that "imagination precedes implementation." Imagination is the engine of social life and entrepeneurship, an engine with enormous power. All human good and evil might be said to spring from it. Synthetic medicines and satellite pictures from Mars are possible because of human imagination, as were the laws created to regulate slavery in North America and the blueprints and train schedules for Auschwitz. The formidable and ambiguous powers of the imagination are integral to humanity, but subject to devastating distortions if disconnected from the compass of conscience and the memory of grief, suffering, and pain. Hannah Arendt is correct: "Lack of imagination keeps people from existing." It robs them of their power.

In a fast-paced, future-oriented, advertising-driven society, memory is short and selective. The stories of parents and grandparents who struggled to provide their children with the basic necessities and the chance of a better future contain precious, energizing memories for their offspring. When stories remain untold, the compass of conscience and memory loses its power to feed the imagination.

The following childhood story of an IAF leader gives powerful voice to the way that memory shapes imagination.

Ms. Angela Telamantes of Southern California Organizing Committee (SCOC) tells the following story about where her passion for organizing comes from. "When I was growing up as a Hispanic child in an Arizona mining town in the 1950s, the public swimming pool was open only to Anglos from Monday through Saturday. On Sunday we were allowed to swim, and after that the 'dirty' water would be changed. They told us that it was because Mexican kids had sores on their feet, but I knew better. That memory never leaves me. Hispanic children have a special place in my heart. They're why I organize today as an adult in Los Angeles."

Social imagination grounded in memories like these are dangerous to the status quo, to the powers that be. They have the potential not only to comfort the afflicted but also to afflict the comfortable. That is, if we remember, and if we keep imagination in creative tension with its conjugal partner.

The conjugal mate of imagination is hope, the human capacity to act in the world now on behalf of the world as it should be. When we forget our history and cannot imagine a changed world, we cannot act with hope to bring that world into existence. Hope ignites action when the struggle for justice exposes intolerable gaps between the two worlds. German theologian Johann B. Metz captures the transformative power of imagination tempered by the memory of suffering: "Enlightenment rationality heavily stressing the centrality of intellect and will must be balanced by a remembrance (anamnetic reason) which informs human kind with the suffering of others. . . . It is only with the landscape of memory and expectation that we have a grounded Hope between the two worlds."[4]

For those who cherish democratic ideals, hope is grounded in a belief in the solidarity and sovereignty of citizens. In the moment when despair most gravely threatened the United States, Abraham Lincoln called the American experiment the "last, best hope for humanity." Democratic hope envisions a political community where power, freedom, opportunity, and accountability reside not with elites or experts, but with everyday, ordinary people. It is anchored in the conviction that the political whole is more than the sum of the parts and must include all but be dominated by none.

For religious people, hope rests on the intuition that humans are not the only ones who care about the gap between the world as it is and the world as it should be. In the Jewish, Christian, and Islamic holy texts, the Creator of the universe repeatedly takes the side of the most vulnerable—the widow, the orphan, and the stranger—against political and economic arrangements that disregard and disrespect their legitimate interests. The spiritual intuition that we are not alone in our efforts to narrow the gap between the two worlds is captured in the famous admonition that we must pray as if everything depends on the Creator, and work as if everything depends on us.

The ground of democratic hope is a belief not in a sovereign state, but rather in a sovereign citizenry. Like religious hope, democratic hope empowers citizens to act for the good with confidence that they are part of a larger whole. As people of faith, human beings draw on one set of traditions in which hope is a core virtue; as citizens we draw on another. Because both of these sources of hope are available, members of religious institutions can stand shoulder to shoulder with those of secular organizations like labor unions, business groups, and civic associations in seeking change in their communities. Citizens and people of faith (and most of you are some form of both) stand on common ground named hope.

In the early 1980s in East Brooklyn, church groups raised seed money and invited the IAF to conduct an organizing drive. The center of the large area chosen was devastated. Its empty, derelict buildings looked more like a bombed-out war zone than anything resembling a community. After some months of organizing work, the sponsoring committee began to grumble, saying "When are you going to do something about these terrible conditions?" In the next training session, the IAF organizer asked those present to put in writing what they would do with the abandoned, vacant land surrounding them if they controlled it. As he read the written responses (some in English, some in Spanish), he found that nearly two-thirds of the black and Latino renters who had responded had imagined homes on the land. Some had drawn modest buildings, some included a backyard barbecue; some had bedrooms for each family member. A seed was being planted, a new beginning was taking root. Two hundred vacant acres were sprouting three-bedroom homes in the imaginations of these people. The spirit of the prophet Nehemiah hovered over these deliberations, urging that Jerusalem's walls be rebuilt. As the ancient text from Proverbs reminds us, "Where there is no vision the people perish."

Under the auspices of East Brooklyn Congregations (EBC), today there are nearly 4,000 single-family Nehemiah homes forming a community of organized people in East Brooklyn. And the Nehemiah approach to creating affordable home ownership for everyone, which was born in the imaginations of working poor people in a church basement amid the desperation of East Brooklyn, has become a model in communities throughout the United States.

It is no coincidence that IAF organizations are often conceived and born in devastated urban locations and written-off rural areas. That's because the demanding work of organizing across the divides of race, religion, and political persuasion is usually initiated only when leaders on the scene reckon that all else has failed. When they realize that no one but them will see to it that their communities develop the political clout and money to change things, the motivation to organize is born. Hope requires intentional, imaginative moves toward a better future, based on clear and conscious knowledge of what really happened in the past. IAF organizations are founded on and cultivate the virtue of hope, because their leaders and organizers understand that as people's hope for a meaningful life ebbs, the tide of nihilistic despair rises.

The fourth polarity in the overall relationship between the world as it is and the world as it should be, then, is the tension between our innate imagination and the inspiration of hope. As with each of the polarities, imagination and hope can flourish only when held in tight relationship to each other. When that tension is maintained, imagination inspires hope for a better world, and hope fires imagination to shape that world.

Being ←——→ Becoming

The tension between the two worlds is a whole; you won't find any of the polarities floating around alone, any more than you can find economics without politics or vice versa. Now that I've broken the tensions between the two worlds down into its components for purposes of analysis, it's time to put the whole back together again. Understanding the overall in-betweenness of the two worlds involves recognizing that human beings live constantly in the dialectic between *being* and *becoming*. Being is a mystery that can only become and continue to become forever. Cardinal Newman said it this way: "To live is to change, and to live well is to have changed often."

The modern philosopher Alfred North Whitehead built his whole explanation of reality on the polarity of being and becoming. His vision of what it takes to be real comes down to two points. First, everything that is, is developing; nothing real is static. Second, development only occurs within the context of relationships. Relationships drive development through nurture and challenge. They are the source of our capacity to initiate, to create, to develop our political selves. The web of relationships is the womb of our development through life; without it we do not come into life nor do we grow and change.

Human beings live, move, and have our being in the tension between the two worlds, between being and becoming. What we might become always contends for our attention and energy with the maintenance of what we have already achieved. People dominated by a concern for being hold new possibilities hostage to past accomplishments. Their futures can only be more of the same. Those preoccupied with becoming, with constant novelty, are unable to draw on the meaning and value of past accomplishments to build new futures. Either of these approaches to life robs us of the creativity that is inherent in our political capacity, as it is in our sexuality. Becoming more fully human requires that we hold what we've already done in proper tension with the new possibilities that imagination brings. The present is where we do that.

Each of the four tensions I described in this chapter is one face of the dialectic of being and becoming. How we deal with all of them determines our overall balance between past accomplishments and future possibilities, between the relentless *is* and the inspiring *ought*. In struggling with the tension between being and becoming, we develop, and we honor those who have gone before us, leaving behind the heritage of vision and values on which we stand, and those who will come after us, standing on our shoulders to create futures that we cannot imagine. The Russian philosopher Nikolay Berdyayev had it right: "The life of personality is not self-preservation of the individual, but self-development and self-determination." Whether we choose it or not, we are always becoming, and radicals realize that.

When the Two-World Tension Is Lost, or The War Over Values

Powerful forces constantly try to undermine the necessary creative tension between the two worlds. When they succeed, we lose our moral compass and are left to choose between two distorted ways to live, so-called realism on one side and so-called idealism on the other.

The Received Culture of Materialism: Domination of the As-Is

The tension between the two worlds may collapse into world-as-it-is values only. Then we get self-serving individualism as a way of life. People become consumers or self-actualizers who dismiss ethics or morality as pious non-sense of no relevance in the real world and operate on the amorality of selfishness and instant gratification.

Self-interest, the prime moving force of human behavior, is distorted into the belief that self-regard and being self-serving are bottom-line winners. The mantra of isolated self-interest is "maximize profits, minimize risk," which shrinks self-interest into selfishness. Real differences don't count, and neither do dreams. Ideals like "E pluribus unum" become empty decorations on monuments and money, as individuals go their separate ways, unable to recognize common interests with others. Public life disappears, as those who can do so retreat into the realm of gated communities, private schools, and independent taxing districts, where each island says to society, "I have no need of you," and "Not in my back yard." The good life portrayed and pushed by Madison Avenue advertising is a shopping mall on a cruise ship. Whoever dies owning the most stuff wins.

Power is understood as domination. Be number one. Use force and violence if necessary. People are objects to be used. Power trumps love. The hard work of resolving difficulties through political engagement is replaced by bribery, coercion, and violence. Instrumental rationality turns people into commodities and colonists, the Earth into raw material, and technology into an idol. Left to itself, the world as it is operates on crass, self-destructive power.

Instant change for its own sake is dangerous. Speed and chaos eliminate distinctions of past, present, and future. No boundaries are allowed in an ever-present here and now. Change is limited to the market-driven fads of entertainment, celebrities, and consumer goods. Reality becomes a kaleidoscope of continually shifting images, in a world where "image is everything." Time and space collapse into an endless here and now in which "anything goes."

Finally, when the tension between the two worlds collapses into materialism, imagination is sacrificed on the altar of high technology and virtual reality. Imagination is reduced to dramatized fantasies, memory to nostalgia for "the good old days" that never were, and hope to putting your money down on the spin of the wheel, the lottery or the online trade. When we forget our roots and traditions, we can't imagine a future worthy of our sacrifices, and are left with only the harried activity of here-and-now consumption.

The world I've just described isn't the real world; it's what we get when we disconnect from our moral center and avoid the tension of the two worlds.

Impotent Idealism: Domination of the Should-Be

A lot of churchy types emphasize the afterlife world. They don't keep the two worlds in balance—in between. They live an otherworldly idealism. These otherworldly types reject the world as it is as corrupt. They hold tight to ideologies, look for miracles, and withdraw from others, especially those different from themselves. Heaven's Gate, the cults of David Koresh and Jim Jones, and those responsible for 9/11 are extreme examples. Such groups long for a make-believe world beyond the present. This is the version of religion that led Marx to indict it as the "opium of the people." Otherworldly leaders make inspiring moral speeches but couldn't organize anything in the real world. The political version of this stance is the cynic who says, "What's the use of fighting city hall? It's all money anyway." "High-road" and puritanical moralities have no tolerance for the messy imperfections and compromises of the world as it is.

Self-sacrifice is distorted into folks lining up to become doormats, victims, or martyrs. People abandon their rightful claims to human dignity and full

participation. Rather than engage in inevitable conflicts and ambiguous bat-
tles with the powers that be, they prefer the self-proclaimed heroism of falling
on their swords. The greatest ethical act, to give one's life for another,
is distorted into a gesture of self-contempt. Self-giving becomes self-
degradation.

Otherworldliness degenerates love into abstract, romantic mush. The inevitable tensions of any authentic relationship are replaced by false, one-sided
concern. Trying to live only for others keeps us from loving well, just as trying
to live only for self keeps us from "powering" well.

The search for unity or harmony works sometimes in music, but rarely in
life. Peace and justice are goals, sometimes approached but rarely realized or
sustained. Compromise is dismissed as betrayal of the purity of one's vision
and values. Politeness masquerading as middle-class civility prevents us from
confronting the rough edges of confrontation and conflict.

Finally, when the tension between the two worlds collapses into false, otherworldly idealism, hope degenerates into selective amnesia about the past
and wishful thinking about the future. This world is despised as evil, sinful,
and corrupt. Hope is reduced to the fantasy of a better world, somewhere,
someday. Whatever awaits us on the other side of death, pie in the sky won't
feed hungry children on Earth today, and heavenly mansions won't protect
them from earthly cold tonight. Hope disconnected from the dangerous
memories of past struggles for change and the realistic imagination of better
futures is toothless and hollow.

Keeping the Two Worlds in Balance

People need guidelines for living in the tension of the two worlds. Parents,
teachers, and religious leaders call those guidelines *morality*. Without moral
guidance we are on the sea of life without boat or paddle, buffeted by the
winds of individualistic consumerism and false idealism. The formation that
young people traditionally receive in their families, congregations, and
schools has stressed the world as it should be ("Treat others as you would
like to be treated," "Do good," "Go along," "Obey authority," "Offer it up,"
"What's worth doing is worth doing right"). While truthful, such teachings
convey a simplistic, overly idealized picture of life in the real world. The life
lessons conveyed by television, movies, and advertising teaches young people
quite a different set of lessons ("If it feels good, do it," "Whoever dies with
the most toys wins," "Greed is good," "Do it to them before they do it to
you," "Image is everything"). The gospel according to Hollywood and Madison Avenue portrays the real world as a materialistic, pleasure-seeking, com-

petitive, and violent rat race, where the name of the game is looking out for number one. Young people whose moral values were formed in the idealism or the absence of family formation, congregations, and schools face a rude shock in their twenties when they discover how rarely the world as it should be is present in public life. Selfishness and materialism coupled with unilateral, coercive power rule the day. Peace and harmony, mercy and justice, are relegated to Sunday islands. The individualistic morality portrayed in entertainment and advertising seems closer to the way things really work.

The massive unilateral power of world capitalism is daily and relentlessly aimed at us and our children through entertainment and advertising, which have been deliberately made harder and harder to separate. Their goal is simple: to create the wants and needs in people that turn us into consumers, beings who cannot be happy without the latest, "hottest" goods and experiences. Consumerism as a way of life prevails when the tension between the two worlds collapses in the direction of the world as it is, and the evil genius of capitalism's marketing includes its ability to steal world-as-it-should-be symbols and use them to sell things in the marketplace. Advertising slogans like "be all that you can be," "reach out and touch someone," and "own a piece of the rock" appeal to important values and symbols from the world as it should be, in an effort to undermine that world by turning human beings into reactors, and wants into needs.

Churches and other should-be organizations usually attempt to counter the materialistic juggernaut by otherworldly means, encouraging their members to come to church, keep their minds on "higher things," and avoid the fray. Or they turn to the enemy's own methods and try to market community and commitment the way others sell perfume or insurance. Is it any wonder that cynicism about religious and democratic institutions abound?

The hard truth is that neither the responsible institutions nor television, movies, and advertising prepare young people for their imminent confrontation with a real world of ambiguity, conflict, mixed motivations, and social sin. Neither a cynical nor a simplistic vision of life can give young people an adequate moral compass for life in the real world. Instead of helping young people to live with integrity and flexibility inside the back-and-forth pull of the four polarities, adults who cannot model living in both worlds and the inevitable tension between them force young people to choose one world and dismiss the other.

Both individualism and idealism are rudderless because they cannot recognize the necessity and legitimacy of "low-road" or pragmatic morality, the demanding, ambiguous ethics of realistic trade-offs in the everyday world as it is. According to the paradigm of the two worlds, immorality is the failure to connect what we must do to survive and thrive in the world as it is with being true to our vision of the world as it should be. Authentic morality or realistic idealism is holding the two worlds in creative tension.

Effective ideals don't move people to the sidelines of life. They are the stars that guide us, our moral compass in navigating the inevitably ambiguous world of power and self-interest. To be moral is to struggle in the arena of the world as it is while guided by the values of the world as it should be, not to go off shopping or trading online or to sit in pews on the sidelines of life saying, "Ain't things awful?" Operating in reality while ignoring values leads to cynicism, division, and coercion. Holding onto values disconnected from the real world robs morality of credibility and relevance. When the tension between the two worlds collapses in either direction, humanity's integrity collapses with it, because we were created to live in-between.

The great poet Goethe's final letter describes the successful life as a "judicious surrender to the natural rhythm of opposing tendencies." Surrendering to the rhythm of the inevitable tension between the two worlds is the true moral destiny of humanity. To do that requires that we develop the social knowledge, courage, and politicalness to live with others inside the polarities of self-interest and self-sacrifice, power and love, change and harmony, and imagination and hope. Taking responsibility for our destiny means deliberately embracing the fearsome, creative tension that comes when we choose to live resolutely in-between the world as it is and the world as it should be, refusing to be condemned either to materialism or false idealism as a way of life. Living well with the two-world tension is *the* root of true radicalism.

2

The Relational Meeting

"Whatever one's philosophical or even theological position, a society is not the temple of value-idols that figure on the front of its monuments or in its constitutional scrolls; the value of a society is the value it places on human relations. . . . To understand and judge a society, one has to penetrate its basic structure to the human bond upon which it is built; this undoubtedly depends upon legal relations, but also upon forms of labor, ways of loving, living, and dying."

MAURICE MERLEAU-PONTY

The Most Radical Thing We Teach

You just finished the main chapter on *why* we organize. This chapter is the key one on *how* we go about doing it. Relational meetings are the glue that brings diverse collectives together and allows them to embrace the tension of living in-between the two worlds. I organized full time for eight years without understanding what I was experiencing or being able to explain it. It was only when I tried to teach others that I had to reflect and outline an approach to building power organizations. To me, the relational meeting is the best IAF offers. Properly understood, it's not a science, not technique, but an art form. It's one organized spirit going after another person's spirit for connection, confrontation, and an exchange of talent and energy.

In the sacred texts of the Abrahamic religions, we find God holding relational meetings at critical moments. The stories of Moses at the burning bush (Exodus 3), Paul on the road to Damascus (Acts 9), and Muhammad in the cave on Mount Hira (Koran 96) are classic accounts of relational meetings called by the Creator that set three spirits on paths that changed the world. When people asked the Buddha in his later years what sort of being he was, he replied, "I am awake." A good relational meeting wakes somebody up.

Modern IAF defines the relational meeting as an encounter that is face to face—one to one—for the purpose of exploring the development of a public relationship. You're searching for talent, energy, insight, and relationships; where these are present you have found some power to add to your public collective. Without hundreds and thousands of such meetings, people cannot forge lasting public relationships based on solid social knowledge or build lasting citizens organizations. Other parts of organizing, like caucuses, conventions, and demonstrations, only have lasting effects if they emerge and take their lead from what happens in relational meetings.

James Madison said, "Great things can only be accomplished in a narrow compass." The IAF relational meeting is narrow in compass—one person face to face with another—but significant in intention. It is a small stage that lends itself to acts of memory, imagination, and reflection. It constitutes a public conversation on a scale that allows space for thoughts, interests, possibilities, and talent to mix. It is where a public newness begins.

A solid relational meeting brings up stories that reveal people's deepest commitments and the experiences that gave rise to them. In fact, the most important thing that happens in good relational meetings is the telling of stories that open a window into the passions that animate people to act. In a relational meeting with an African-American leader, an organizer asked why she seemed so willing to take risks, why she was willing to step up and lead when others held back. She is, by nature, a shy woman, not at ease in the public arena, happier in her home and among her family members. In response to this simple but pointed question, she told the following story.

When I was a young girl in North Carolina, my sister and I began to attend the local Roman Catholic church. In those days, blacks sat in the back pews. Now I was a very large young girl, rather heavy, and so was my sister. When we went to that church, I saw no reason why my sister and I should sit in the back. So one Sunday we went right up and sat in the first pew. The pastors and ushers were upset. The pastor came over before Mass and asked me if we would please sit in the back, like all other blacks. I was scared as I could be, but I just couldn't see where God would care where we sat, so I said no. Finally, the ushers came and carried me and my sister to the back. Carried us right down the aisle of the church.

On the next Sunday, my sister and I sat in the front pew again, and the priest came and the ushers came and they hauled us off again, huffing and puffing. On the third Sunday, the same thing happened. By this time, we were pretty well known. Two black girls who got carried away to the back of the church every Sunday. My family, my mother particularly, was frightened at what we were doing, but she said we were doing the right thing.

On the fourth Sunday, the priest and ushers didn't do a thing. The Mass started, the choir sang, we took our seats, and from then on we sat where we wanted in that church and in any Roman Catholic church we ever attended.

After tens and hundreds of relational meetings, every experienced IAF leader and organizer carries in his or her memory a set of precious stories like the one you just read, stories that sustain us through difficult and often thankless work.

Discovering a New Foundation for Organizing

Beginning in Chicago's racially polarized neighborhoods in the late 1950s and early '60s, Dick Harmon and I crafted the art of the relational meeting in the streets and taught it to organizers in Saul Alinsky's training institute. Saul's way of organizing, which we had inherited, was influenced by electoral politics and the CIO labor organizing of John L. Lewis. In this approach, where one person equals one vote and all votes are equal, the ability to mobilize large numbers of people is the key. Under Alinsky, organizing meant "pick a target, mobilize, and hit it." In the modern IAF, it's "connect and relate to others." Issues follow relationships. You don't pick targets and mobilize first; you connect people in and around their interests. The inspiration for most of the best public tactics I've ever created came from relational meetings.

It was a chilly Friday night in the fall of 1959 in Chicago's racially changing St. Sabina's neighborhood on the Southwest Side. I had asked for and finally got the name of a key bomb thrower committed to keeping Negro families from moving into the all-white neighborhood. When I called the person whose name I had, he suspiciously agreed that I could come by at 9:30.

It was dark when I nervously rang the doorbell of a small white bungalow. I was greeted with "Let's go to the kitchen," where four items were prearranged on the table—a full bottle of Jim Beam, two shot glasses, and a pistol. I began the meeting by pointing out that violence just frightened white mothers, who put up "For Sale" signs the next morning. "They're not gonna raise their kids on a battlefield," I told him. His response was to have a shot and, as he raised his glass to his lips, he made it clear that I was to do the same.

About a half hour passed this way, when the back door screeched opened suddenly, and three big guys silently walked in and joined the meeting, standing. The house's owner said, "Have another shot and tell them what you're telling me." After two or three minutes of my analysis, one of the standing guys interrupted me with, "This guy is a nigger lover." I sensed that the relational meeting was over, and I was next.

Instinctively, I countered (where it came from, I'll never know), "You guys are stupid. You don't even know who pays me to do this full-time." Then I volunteered, "Monsignor P. J. Molloy of St. Leo's [a tough, keep-'em-out local priest]. Let's call him now," I said, motioning toward the telephone.

We went back and forth for another hour and a half. Finally, I stood and said, "I gotta go." I left to silence and wobbled to my car but was alert enough to check underneath it then, and every day for the next two weeks, before starting it.

The beginnings of the IAF relational meeting weren't churchy or academic, but in places like that kitchen on the Southwest Side of Chicago.

After engaging in 250 or 300 relational meetings in the mid-1950s on the racially changing Southwest Side of Chicago, it dawned on me that I had stumbled onto a very useful tool, something that Alinsky had not figured out. These dialogues had provided me with a blueprint for organizing toward a free and open society, a way to break through racial segregation democratically. Here was an alternative to violence, disruption, and fear. It wasn't until I was confronted in the late 1960s with creating a training institute that I fully digested this experience. Teaching rookies how to organize through the selective, systematic use and careful evaluation of relational meetings made me realize that I had discovered a treasure. Building on the social knowledge I had gained under Alinsky during the 1950s allowed me to teach and develop the relational meeting in the 1960s. For the last forty years, senior IAF organizers have modeled the art form for trainees. In local and national training, leaders have been taught to do them. We have come to understand the relational meeting as the basic tool for all effective broad-based organizations.

Laying the Foundation for a Broad-Based Citizens Organization

In the process of constructing a broad-based citizens organization, thousands of one-on-one meetings will be held.

Upon returning to Chicago to build a broad-based organization in 1994, I did half a dozen relational meetings with a charismatic priest who had started with Alinsky forty years earlier. Fifteen minutes into the sixth one, I sensed an old man with old connections, old stories; a worn-down veteran, but still having lots of passion. Painfully, I took a risk and followed my instincts. I said, "The problem, Jack, is you. You can't be center stage. The young priests can't develop—you're in the way." His face dropped. I paused. After a minute or two he said, "Ed, what should I do?" I said, "Give me the names of 12 to 15 successful young pastors in the city and suburbs." "Why the suburbs?" he asked. "It won't work without them," I answered. This painful relational meeting had triggered in me the next step. Three months later we had the nucleus of a sponsoring committee, with Monsignor Jack Egan, the IAF treasurer, on the sidelines, where he stayed until he died.

In bringing the United Power organization to birth in metropolitan Chicago from 1995 to 1997, the organizers and initial leaders conducted 9,000 to 9,500 relational meetings over two years; about 25 percent of those were duds. Every good meeting in the bunch involved relational power, intentionality, and mutual recognition. Holding a number of relational meetings on a weekly basis is the main work leaders must do to sustain and develop their organization. The relational encounter is the radical source of all successful solidarity in a democratic society.

The relational meeting is a thirty- to thirty-five-minute opportunity to set aside the daily pressures of family, work, and deadlines to focus deliberately upon another person, to seek out their talent, interest, energy, and vision. Don't violate this time frame. People do that all the time because they want conversation or chitchat. There are shelves full of books on how to keep people talking. No matter how interesting it is, don't violate the thirty-minute rule. In a relational meeting, you're checking people out, piquing their curiosity, and looking for talent, not for friends or "dialogue." Time discipline will help keep you focused on public business. If the first thirty minutes goes well, don't keep going—schedule another meeting. In the meantime, check out the people they send you to. If they're duds, don't go back. The relational meeting is an art form that forces you to work within a time frame. Something in the nature of these meetings requires discipline about time. These are moments of intensity that cannot be sustained.

Here's a piece of social knowledge for you on time and power. In relational meetings with big power people, they'll keep the first twenty to twenty-five minutes on you. Ordinary people will let you keep the focus on them for the first twenty to twenty-five minutes, then they'll want to know something about what makes you tick and what you want from them. If you don't believe me, try it. That's how you get social knowledge.

The implication of asking for a relational meeting is that the other person's perspective is of value, that listening to the stories and insights, the memories and struggles, of another is more important than hustling their name for a petition or getting them out to vote. In contrast to prestructured, carefully controlled and impersonal strategies like opinion surveys and focus groups, the relational meeting is a risky, reciprocal event. The relational meeting is a two-way street. The person requesting such a meeting isn't a sponge, soaking up information about the other person's life. He or she must be prepared to be vulnerable about his or her own social passions, values, frustrations, and concerns because inside relational meetings, people will turn the tables with their own questions:

- Who are you?
- What do you want?
- Why do you do what you do?
- Who pays you?
- Are you running for office?

Effective leaders in their own right will want to know something about what makes *you* tick. They will test, probe, and agitate you. You need to be able to reciprocate, to have the ego, clarity, and flexibility to respond to someone else's initiatives. That's why we need to see the relational meeting not as a rigid structure but as a plastic form that can be bent, shaped, and changed spontaneously in response to unpredictable demands and possibilities. No two relational meetings are alike.

While the dominant culture tells us that cell phones, beepers, fax machines, e–mail, and Internet chat rooms have made face-to-face communication obsolete, organizers and leaders who regularly do the intense work of relational meetings understand that these disciplined conversations touch our depths in a unique and irreplaceable way, even if one never sees the other person again. In relational meetings, the "why" questions so often avoided by people have a space in which to surface.

- Why are things like this?
- Why am I doing what I do?
- Why don't I spend more time on what I *say* is most important to me?

Having these disciplined, existential dialogues is no waste of time; it is one of the highest and most valuable ways to spend our time. There is no electronic substitute. There is no chance for community without the relational meeting.

The Art of the Relational Meeting

A relational meeting isn't selling or pushing an issue or membership in an organization. We must listen rather than talk and ask questions based on what we are hearing. What is the other person thinking and feeling? What makes them tick? What's their number-one priority? Your basic tools for the meeting are your eyes, ears, nose, instinct, and intuition.

Short succinct questions are the key.

- Why do you say that?
- How so?
- What's that mean to you?
- How come it matters?

You must be prepared to interrupt with brief, tight questions like these, but not to make your own speeches. Once you ask a probing question, shut up and listen, and be alert for the next question. The artistry of relational meetings has to do with this in-and-out movement.

In relational meetings, we look for interests, talents, and connections across the spectrum of race, class, religion, and politics. Those who initiate them are particularly alert for people in the "moderate middle" of the political spectrum, who must be found in large numbers to form the core of an effective broad–based organization. The relational meeting is the entry point to public life. It is never done merely "to get to know" another person. Face-to-face meetings that lead to the development of an ongoing public relationship form the core of collective action for the common good.

The relational meeting isn't chitchat, like the usual informal exchange over coffee or drinks. In casual meetings, we take people as they present themselves. We don't push. We don't dig. We don't ask why or where a notion came from. We don't probe an idea. We don't raise possibilities. We don't ask questions that engage the imagination: "Well, what if you looked at it this way?" "How would your parents have reacted?" "How would you feel if you were the other person?" In everyday, casual talk, we don't show depth of curiosity or interest, and we don't expect curiosity and interest to be demonstrated toward us. Those who become proficient in holding public relational meetings learn that they must be "on" while they do them—intentional, focused, and prepared to agitate and be agitated in turn.

The relational meeting is not voyeuristic. It's not an occasion to pry into the private life of the other person. The difference between prying and probing is important. When people pry, they show excessive curiosity; they try to force the other person open. Curiosity becomes an indiscriminate end in itself. A probe is more focused. It is an attempt to find the other's center.

In a relational meeting, probing reveals the underpinnings of someone's public action or inaction. If a neighborhood resident is angry about the abandoned building on the block and has attempted to organize others but stopped short of direct action, it's important to discover why. The personal reasons that motivate action are revealed in stories: a grandfather who immigrated during the Depression to establish a family in America; a mother who served as a model of courage and strength during the anxiety and deprivation of wartime; a brother gone bad who exerts a negative pull that the person is resisting. Stories like these don't rest on the surface, to be picked up in casual chatter. Only concerted and intentional encounters will bring them to light.

The relational–meeting approach is selective. Unless I get fooled, I have relational meetings with leaders only. And I go up the food chain, toward more power. You can't get to power without a credential.

In 1986 while on an organizing trip to Johannesburg, South Africa, I requested and got a relational meeting with newly elected Archbishop Desmond Tutu. It was friendly enough, but the archbishop was agitated by the refusal of President Botha to meet with him. After several minutes of listening to him, I said, "If I were Botha [God forbid], I wouldn't meet with you either." He spit out, "Why do you say that?" I said, "Because if he recognized you, he might have to recognize all the other black South Africans." Apartheid wouldn't allow white power to recognize blacks. Boldly, I said, "You should have had 10,000 black South Africans outside the Johannesburg Cathedral when you were made a bishop in the Anglican Church." He responded, "We had some blacks present in the cathedral." "Bishop," I said, "had you come out after the installation and addressed 10,000 black Anglicans militantly, Botha might have given you a meeting."

Archbishop Tutu and I parted on friendly terms, but that was a confrontational relational meeting. I had challenged him on power, courage, and not understanding the opposition's interests.

Why have relational meeting with leaders only? First, a leader is someone with relationships who can deliver his or her followers. The point of relational meetings in broad-based organizing is to find leaders and connect them up, not to duplicate preexisting relationships or replace leaders. Second, people who are followers will tend to dump their problems on you, which is deenergizing for you. Interested followers will be invited to assemblies and actions and be given the opportunity to grow into leaders inside a broad-based organization over time, but you can't build an organization of organizations around followers. In real estate, the mantra is "location, location, location." With relational meetings, it's "selection, selection, selection." If you get caught with a follower, there's an easy way out. Just say, "Take me to your leader."

The relational meeting is not a search for those who share our faith, class, politics, or other views. Ideologues on the right or left tend to seek consistency and certainty. The disaffection with electoral politics of the vast moderate middle of American society is in large part a reaction to the increasing insularity and narrowness of far-out liberals and right-wing conservatives. Both groups end up preaching to their ideological clubs, using their own language, their own fabricated theology, and their own single agendas. Both extremes communicate, "If you want to join us, you have to be like us—follow the party line." Neither extreme sends the message that its agenda has some fluidity, that its tone or strategy might be altered, that newcomers are expected to bring something to the group's agenda. Neither group does much organizing, in the sense that the term is used in these pages. Instead, they pressure people by means of direct mail, television ad campaigns, op-ed pieces, focus groups, and market research studies, with an ever watchful eye on public opinion polls. But polls cannot measure people's intensity or passion for change, nor can they bring people into real relationships.

Finally, the relational meeting is not a technique or an electronic shortcut, but an art form. Relational meetings aren't social science surveys for gathering data, or one more focus group for dissecting the public. In sharp contrast to the purpose of isolated and arbitrary opinion polling, relational meetings let us discover something of the wholeness or spirit of the others.

- Who are they?
- Who are their heroes and heroines?
- Whom don't they like?
- What is their dream for their family or congregation or neighborhood?
- What would they call a life well lived?
- Can they deliver their institution?
- Are they open to public life and organization?
- Do they have some appetite for action?

Like art, the relational meeting has a certain form and requires certain skills. But relational meetings have to be used flexibly and creatively by those initiating the meetings rather than following a rote method in a formalized manner. Those who become skilled in the art of the relational meeting have learned to use their whole selves—body and spirit, charms, compassion, wits, humor, and anger—in these intense, focused encounters.

To summarize these points, the relational meeting

- is for the purpose of developing a public relationship
- focuses on the spirit and values of the other
- requires an intentional focus that goes beyond ordinary conversation
- necessitates probing and agitating the depths of the other
- demands a measure of vulnerability on both sides
- applies selectively, with leaders only
- bridges the barriers of race, religion, class, gender, and politics
- is a form of art that requires patient development and use of particular skills

When a good relational meeting occurs, two people connect in a way that transcends ordinary, everyday talk. Both have the opportunity to pause and reflect on their personal experience regarding the tension between the world as it is and the world as it should be. And in that moment, a new public relationship may be born, through which both will gain power to be truer to their best selves, to live more effectively and creatively in–between the two worlds. Most of the tactics for action that I've come up with in the last fifty years came partly from something somebody said during a relational meeting.

After the Meeting

At the end of the individual meeting, the leader or organizer asks herself or himself some serious questions.

- Does this person have any animating passion about the state of our world as it is or as it ought to be?
- Does he or she have any anger, grief, memory, and vision about the state of our public life?
- What about a sense of humor?
- Is there a healthy tension between his or her values and reality?
- Did the person ask me anything or exhibit any curiosity about me? Was he or she properly wary of my reasons for seeking a meeting? Was he or she skeptical?
- Would personal problems in family or work prevent this person from participating in and contributing to a collective?

- What would he or she bring to the building of an organization of organizations?
- Who are the person's connections? To whom did he or she refer me?
- Is this person integrated—able to cross racial, religious, and class lines?
- Was there the beginning of some trust or liking between us?
- Is this someone I should contact again next month or forget?
- How should I follow up?

Developing the disciplined habit of setting aside a brief time for careful reflection on questions like these and jotting down a few key words in a notebook or on index cards to be reviewed before the next meeting is critical to reap maximum benefit from the time and energy involved in scheduling and carrying out relational meetings. Otherwise, after 50 relational meetings, you'll forget what happened in meeting number sixteen.

A Challenge to You

The relational meeting is a sophisticated approach to effective organizing in any area of life. It's simple, but it's not easy. It's a small stage on which the two worlds of is and ought come together for a moment. If the tension between the two worlds that I laid out in the previous chapter, and the possibility of relational meetings in this one, have captured your imagination, the next step is to develop your experience-based social knowledge of the relational meeting. To do this, you must act. Ask for a meeting with someone outside your usual circle of family and friends. Give yourself a credential. Make a phone call to get a date and time at the other person's convenience. Take thirty minutes to seek out that person's interests and values as they relate to the larger community you both share. Be prepared to be open about your own concerns and priorities. When the meeting is over, use the questions above to reflect on what happened. Imagine the person you met with in a collective with others acting for change on some issue that touches his or her self-interest.

After about thirty of these meetings, you'll begin to get the idea. Why not try it? What's the worst thing that could happen? They throw you out! Get a public life. Take a risk. You may like it.

3

Broad-Based Organizing: An Intentional Response to the Human Condition

"Politics, like sexuality, is an activity which must be carried on; one does not create it or decide to join in—one simply becomes more and more aware that one is involved in it as part of the human condition."

BERNARD CRICK

The Human Condition

Rooted between the material and the spiritual, between the world as it is and the world as it should be, the complexity of the human condition shades into mystery. Nonetheless, its basic plot is simple: We are born with capacities for power and love; we must live with all kinds of people; we will die—so what have we got to lose?[1]

With every birth, a new source of creativity comes into the world. While all human beings have something in common, no two of us are alike. As finite creatures, our existence is time-limited, and we will die. The interplay of creativity, diversity, and limits underlies the struggles, successes, and failures of human existence. All human action and growth—in our families, careers, and community involvements—take place within this existential triad: natality, plurality, and mortality. Let's take a look at each one.

Natality

Like other creatures, human beings survive physically through genes or native instincts. Since Freud we have been frightened by instinct. The so-called "sixth sense" should be honored along with intellect, will, imagination, and other respected characteristics. My life experience has led me to teach that most people have good instincts but hesitate to follow them. Risk-takers, inventors, entrepeneurs, and radicals follow their instincts. We are not only gifted with instincts but also plunged at birth into a social and cultural world shaped by those who came before us. We must internalize and evaluate that world using our critical intelligence. The philosopher Henri Bergson put it this way: "Intelligence and instinct are turned in different directions—intelligence toward matter, instinct toward life."[2] Through our intelligence and instincts, we will further shape what we inherit, leaving a better or worse world for those who follow. Men and women make history.

In the great mystery of co-creation, we bring children into the world. Mothers and fathers create new, unique persons. A passage from a novel by Bernard McClaverty registers this newness through a mother's eyes.

> It was so utterly common and ordinary. And yet when it happened it was a miracle. That her baby should be here, that she should be who she was, was a profound mystery. . . . Her child was so much more than Catherine's eyes could take in. Although what she saw astonished her. The fingernails, the dark fluffy hair of the head, the whorl of the ear, they were all part of her and yet they belonged to someone else. Somebody totally other.[3]

A birthing room is totally changed by the arrival of a new embodied spirit, a full person with their own needs, feelings and style. The ability to generate newness, to make new beginnings, of which bringing a child into the world is the most wonderful expression, is what philosopher Hannah Arendt called *natality*. She describes this newness as "the beginning which came into the world when we were born and to which we respond by beginning something new on our own initiative."[4]

Natality enables people to initiate, to create new potentials. In public life, that is the politicalness, or active power for social change, that I've already described. The way things are and the way they could be confront each other. Action is the capacity humans have to initiate efforts to narrow the gap between the is and the ought. Action marks the difference between dynamic living and rotting away in the status quo. The relational meetings I laid out in the previous chapter and the public actions I'll discuss in Chapter Five are the two most basic ways of exercising and practicing natality in real life.

In adopting the Declaration of Independence, the founding fathers of the United States of America made their understanding of the importance of natality or newness clear:

> We hold these truths to be self-evident, that all Men are created equal, that they are endowed by their Creator with certain unalienable Rights, that among these are Life, Liberty, and the Pursuit of Happiness. That to

secure these Rights, Governments are instituted among Men, deriving their just powers from the Consent of the Governed. That whenever any Form of Government becomes destructive of these Ends, it is the Right of the People to alter or abolish it, and to institute new Government, having its Foundation on such Principles and organizing its Powers in such Form, as to them shall seem most likely to affect their Safety and Happiness.

When our government does not work, such as when the Supreme Court picks a president or corporate money and lobbyists place oil and gas above the well-being of our children, education, and low-income protection, it is the responsibility of citizens to exercise their natality by using their political-ness to organize. When the founders spoke of the right of people "to alter or abolish" their government, they were acknowledging the place of natality, radical newness.

Natality is at the core for people of faith, too. The Abrahamic religions consider the human person to have been created in the image and likeness of the God of Moses, Jesus, and Muhammad. Recall the famous text of Genesis 1:27, sacred to all three traditions, in which we read, "So God created humans in his own image, in the image of God he created them; male and female He created them." Another classic proclamation of natality is found in the He-brew scriptures when God, speaking through the prophet Isaiah, proclaims, "Behold, I am doing a new thing; now it springs forth, do you not perceive it? I will make a way in the wilderness and rivers in the desert" (Isaiah 43:19).

In Arendt's words, "The new always happens against the overwhelming odds of statistical laws and their probability, which for all practical, everyday purposes amounts to certainty. . . ."[5] The new surprises. Through action, human natality makes ways in the wilderness and rivers in the desert, bringing changes to the world as it is that experts could not imagine. Creations like the steam engine, electricity, the automobile, nuclear power, and the Internet, as well as the mixing of cultures being forced on us by globalization, demand that society stretch beyond previous limits. Through our human natality, the "impossible" happens.

Margarita Vargas stood on the stage, looked out onto the sea of 7,000 faces in the Shrine Auditorium, saw the lights from the TV cameras, and felt her knees buckle. As she stood ready to kick off a huge cam-paign to raise the minimum wage in California, Margarita realized that nothing in her background had prepared her for such a moment—nothing except the three years of training she had received as an IAF leader.

Born in Mexico, Vargas had spent the last twenty years raising her eight children, just as her mother and grandmother had done. Although she had moved to the United States with her husband before the first baby was born, she had never found it necessary to learn English or become a citizen. But when her youngest child was three and the family moved to Baldwin Park, California, she found herself wanting more.

At the urging of a friend, she went to a special meeting at her church. Sitting quietly in the back of the room, she looked around. There were people there she had never associated with before: blacks, whites, Protestants, Jews. She couldn't understand everything that was going on, but she did understand that this diverse group of people wanted to do something to make the community better. Vargas had some ideas, but she was too shy and unsure of her English to speak up. Still, she continued to come to the meetings, because she was thrilled to see ordinary people taking power—power that she had thought belonged only to those in authority: government officials, corporate leaders, and the wealthy.

The stories of IAF organizations and people throughout these pages confirm that human natality does give rise to public birth-moments. Such events require a determined willingness to live with the tension between limitations and possibilities in meaningful action, to embrace the tension of the two worlds.

Plurality

Contrary to the individualism of the received culture, the self's affinity is not to itself in isolation, but to others. The realm of human affairs is rich and complex, ambiguous and tragic, because the others with whom we must work out a shared existence are not just like us. People's perspectives, interests, values, and priorities are unique to them. There is no generic "humanity" except in the realm of abstraction. In reality, people are similar but not the same; they differ, and these differences are dealt with for better and for worse in relationships. This dimension of the human condition is called *plurality*. Whenever two or more human beings are gathered, differences in experience, interests, values, and power will be present. Arendt writes, "We are all the same, that is, human, in such a way that nobody is ever the same as anyone else who ever lived, lives or will live."[6] The plurality or diversity of humanity leaves people with a simple, momentous choice: Do they handle their differences through politicalness or through force and violence? Ever increasing globalization is forcing us to confront our plurality.

Since the time of cave-dwellers, people have had the strong habit of seeking security by congregating with those who are like them. This instinct becomes social sin when it hardens into assuming that one group's way is superior to the ways of others, with an accompanying habit of treating everybody else as inferiors. The "-isms" that plague us, like racism and sexism, are antipluralistic and, thus, antihuman.

Living with plurality requires moving from a fixed world of certainties ("Obey your parents," "Go to church," "Do good, " "Our way is the only way") to facing the ambiguity of the world as it is. This means changing our focus from so-called autonomy to relationship and collective action; from separations (body/soul, self/other, them/us) to organic, yin-yang unity; from autonomous individualism to community and collective action; from static, fixed patterns to reorganizing and transforming; and from quantifiable, scientific knowledge to social, experiential knowledge. People who insist on certainty don't do well in the pluralistic public world of broad-based organizing. Participation in a diverse collective will test your certainties and change them. Going into public action with others in a diverse collective transforms people's lives. Unfortunately, most of us don't get to taste that.

Facing plurality means coming out from behind the barriers that we have inherited around race, religion, class, culture, and gender in search of public relationships based in mutual interest and respect. It means connecting with others where they are; meeting them where they live, work, and pray; venturing onto unfamiliar ground. And this requires forays out of familiar enclaves into "foreign" territory. The plurality of the world demands that people mix their energy, interests, and resources with others if their goal is to build a broad base of power to act collectively. Plurality is of the essence in broad-based organizing, because it can produce a base of organized people power, which no single issue or group can match. The haves don't want to see diverse groups organized. The haves understand the power that creates and want to keep groups divided so that they can keep control. Organized plurality can take on organized money and win.

Mortality

We all know we will die, but nobody knows when. Human beings begin to move toward physical death at the instant of birth. Existence on Earth will come to an end. This dimension of the human condition is *mortality*. Mortality means you have a funeral waiting. The earthly life, which is a gift, is limited in time and space. Augustine put it clearly: "When we finally lay down, we lay down for a long time." Only facing death squarely can free people of the illusion that there's always more time and inspire them to really live their lives. Whether people integrate their mortality or run from it through avoidance and distractions has a lot to do with what the quality of their lives will be.

Accepting mortality means deciding what you want on your tombstone. Failing to face the fact of death leaves people unfocused, scattered, and prey to the endless stream of fads and addictions purveyed by the materialistic received culture. Time "gets away" from us. Facing Augustine's hard truth makes us focus our attention and energize our living, as the following reflections by an IAF organizer make plain.

> When my father was dying of cancer, I sat many hours with him, talking to him about his own life. My father never completed the eighth grade and was bitterly frustrated at his own lack of accomplishment. He worked hard all his life and did the best he could, but his hopes and dreams were never realized because he did not have the opportunities to fulfill his potential. He ran out of time.
>
> My father's feelings at the end of his life ignited a realization in me. It dawned on me that organizing is about more than winning on issues—it is about developing people's potential to realize their hopes. A focus on developing people changes your sense of time. Issue campaigns involve a relatively short span of time—weeks, months, a year or two at most. But if your concern is developing people, you need the time frame of a parent—twenty years, a generation. Organizing must be generational.

Confronting limits means more than acknowledging that we will run out of time. It also requires learning to live with the limitations of the world. The mature acceptance of life's inevitable messiness and imperfection forces you to live deliberately between the extremes of cynicism and ideological purity. In public life, this requires that organized citizens and people of faith seek out and initiate opportunities to embody cherished values like living wages for all workers, while accepting the fact that no perfect realization of them is possible. Such people are willing to seek compromises with integrity. They refuse to let the best drive out the better. They'll take half a loaf, if that's all that's possible in the circumstances. They accept their limitations.

Human life is continually shaped by the three existential facts I just described: We create, we are unique, and we die. Natality, plurality, and mortality are not separate compartments inside us. They are woven together in a seamless web, like past, present, and future. Plurality spins directly out of natality. Every human life is not only new but also unique and irreplaceable. For those who realize that time flies on the way to death, relationships move to the center of life, and collective action with others who are different is recognized as the engine and oxygen that lets us spend the limited time we have creatively. If we want to develop our capacities for being creative, embracing differences, and facing the limits of our existence, we must have an instrument and a place in which to do that. In IAF that instrument is the broad-based citizens organization, and the place where it's built is called civil society.

Civil Society, the State, and the Market

The place where people come together voluntarily to act in and around shared interests is called civil society. Contrary to the usual jargon, civil society is the first and critical sector, not the so-called "third sector." The cave, family, and tribe came first. Civil society is the first and most important level of institutions. Its power is generational. It's where values and traditions are instilled and fostered. The state and the market came later and exist to support it.

Civil society trumps the state and the market in value, but most people don't think of it that way. Totalitarians like Stalin, Hitler, and Mao wiped out civil-society institutions right off the bat. Civil society is the political conscience and benchmark of democracy. Wipe it out and anything goes. The organizations of civil society are so-called mediating institutions—families, congregations, schools, social clubs, citizens organizations, athletic groups, parent-teacher associations, block clubs, unions, fraternal and social organizations, and so on. They are usually small units of power, constituted by organized people with their own money. These institutions are the glue that holds societies together. Without these relationships and this power, there is chaos and anarchy. Civil-society institutions pass on the meanings and virtues necessary for human, political life. If civil society is fatally weakened, neither the family nor the state nor the market can survive. That's why we need safety nets like social security, free education, health care, and living wages for all citizens.

In strong civil-society institutions, relationships revolve around something other than buying and selling and voting every few years. Self and other meet as unique, irreplaceable persons. Such relationships are the source of the most sacred meanings in human life because it is within them that people are connected to their place and roots, learning the stories, imbibing the customs and traditions, and discovering the vocations that give their lives meaning and value. It's here that we become persons, rather than mere consumers or voters. Here, people are not reduced to statistics, market segments, or job descriptions. They are known and know others by face, one to one. Their presence is recognized, and their absence is felt.

The state includes official governments at local, state, regional, national, and international levels. Its primary functions are enforcing law and order within its boundaries, creating a social safety net for its citizens, and providing for the common defense against outside threats. In order to carry those out, it controls money and collects taxes from the people. The state's networks include civil-service employees, academic elites, and party operatives hired to advise on and lobby for government policies and initiatives. The attention span of state operatives is the next election. If ordinary people participate in the state at all, they do so through the ever more minimally political act called voting. The majority of Americans choose not to vote. When I do, I hold my nose.

The market includes all the institutions of business and commerce. Its reason for being is to generate profits through the production and distribution of goods and services. Its touchstone for creating those profits is efficiency through the careful, constant calculation of the costs and benefits associated with particular decisions. Market calculations create commodities for whatever sale prices the market will bear. The key market institution is the corporation, a legal fiction with the same rights as a person, which shields its officers and employees from personal culpability for the corporation's acts. Unlike persons, corporations have no natural mortality; their longevity is determined by their adaptability to market conditions. In contrast to the national boundaries of the state, the market is global in scope and reach. It knows no boundaries. While this has been true as long as international trade has existed, the global character and power of the market is expanding exponentially as the result of new technologies and international trade policies. The "new world order" so far is just a new market order. People and the common good are not even on the screen. The focus of the market is the profitable creation and distribution of goods and services. The time frame of the market is always now, this ninety-day earnings period, this quarter's rate of return. Ordinary people participate in the market as workers, clients, customers, and consumers.

For purposes of understanding, it's useful to break out the three basic components of a society as I just did, but every actual society is a blend of state, market, and civil society. In the world as it is, the three sectors blend into and out of one another. Economics and politics—the market and the state—are always interrelated. There is no economy without a political system, and vice versa. In a healthy and just society, state and market power exist in creative tension, creating accountability by constantly challenging each other's proper competence and responsibility. One job of the state is to put boundaries on the market—in other words, to hold it accountable for the common and collective good.

Civil society makes its contribution to humankind by being sufficiently well organized, meaning powerful enough, to hold the elected leaders of the state and the public officials they appoint, as well as the moguls of the market, accountable for the impact of their decisions on individuals, families, and local communities. Arthur Okun, former head of the Federal Reserve, had it right: "The market has its place, but it must be kept in its place." Keeping the market in its place will not happen without broad-based organizing of the institutions of civil society.

The focus of civil society is the well-being of persons, families, and the city. The time perspective of civil society is that of this generation and the next: What must we do now so that the life chances of our grandchildren will be enhanced? When ordinary people participate in civil society, they do so as people of belief committed to public justice and mercy, as citizens committed to the practice of democracy. When the state doesn't keep the market in its place, but instead gets bought by it, as we see all around us in the era of Enron, Tyco, and WorldCom, civil society is all that's left to initiate change.

Broad-Based Citizens Organizations

Broad-based citizens organizations like those of the IAF are twenty-first-century civil-society institutions *par excellence*. Their members are not individuals but mediating institutions—congregations, civic associations, labor unions, and some businesses—that come together to act in concert with others on their respective interests and values in matters of common concern. IAF organizations create the space in which people can think, develop their public life, and be loyal to what they cherish. Collectives of voluntary, mediating institutions are the most progressive social instruments now available for the development of effective politicalness by everyday ordinary citizens. The term "broad-based" is used here to contrast IAF organizations with "community organizations." The latter tend to have a narrow, individual-membership base, operate within a limited turf or neighborhood, and focus on small problems.

We need a little history to understand why twenty-first-century IAF organizations are called broad-based citizens organizations. The early IAF built strong, turf-based, community organizations with clear geographic boundaries, not broad-based collectives. In those days, IAF did not understand the concept or have the organizers to build broad-based organizations on a size and scale that the times demanded. The kind of community organizing IAF did initially was great for a small piece of city turf but was ineffective against huge corporations with political connections bought with money and arranged by good lobbyists.

In the 1980s, IAF started changing the size and scale of organizing. We began to build broader and deeper organizations. We recognized moderates and the middle class as untapped potential. Organizing only poor people couldn't produce enough power. Large citywide or countywide geographic areas were targeted. We held on to Saul Alinsky's insight of building new organizations from the pockets of power that institutions already in the field represent. As a new generation of talented men and women organizers gained confidence and experience, they sought out and engaged all faiths, races, and classes. The poor, working class, middle class, and—to the horror of some ideologues—the wealthy and successful came on board.

IAF affiliates are organizations of other organizations. Individuals need not apply. When you have many small, scattered wheels, you need to create a big wheel out of them. The collective leadership of an organization is trained in the culture of effective, efficient public life. Their operative belief is that democratic justice is never handed to people but must be fought for and attained by public struggle. Because there is no nice, polite way to get change, new organizations must expect frequent confrontation and conflict. Unlike the peace and harmony we expect in private life, a public-life organization intentionally creates tension, targets, and exchanges of power as means to democratic justice. Because an IAF organization is finally about relationality, the relational meeting is its most radical tool.

Broad-based power organizations must be able to take on multiple issues because their member organizations have multiple interests. While an effective organization will ordinarily go into action only on one major issue at a time, it will always have other fights in the bank. An organization's leaders and organizers can never be totally focused on the current issue. They must always be asking the question, "What do we do after we win this one?" The fight in the bank is the next priority issue on which research is being done in preparation for the next struggle. An effective broad-based organization's life has a rhythm of planning, action, and reflection.

In a broad-based collective, member institutions do not function subordinately, like Catholic parishes within a diocese. Instead, each institution retains its identity, mission, and independence, renewing its dues-paying membership in the collective from year to year as long as its involvement serves its interests and expresses its values. By coming together and mixing their talent, time, money, and values, the institutions that make up a broad-based organizations become a civil-society force for state and market powers to reckon with.

IAF collectives exist to act for justice with power by using sound political judgment. By contrast, service and maintenance organizations in health care, education, and religion are aimed not at justice but rather at service and mercy. The effect of their work is to ameliorate the status quo. They tend to ignore power. There are hundreds of thousands of service and maintenance organizations in the United States, but fewer than 100 broad-based citizens organizations. Broad-based collectives are the most potent social instrument now available for the development of politicalness because they are of a size and scale appropriate to countering the market's threat to overwhelm the state.

How to Spot an IAF Organization

You can spot an IAF civil-society organization by several benchmarks. For starters, it will be a dues-based operation. It is not subsidized by local, state, or federal government. It is not dependent upon foundation money or other outside funds. It begins with approximately two years' work by a sponsoring committee, which raises seed money for a serious organizing drive. After creating that breathing space, a broad-based organization will build itself over generations, continually organizing and reorganizing itself.

IAF affiliates are dues-based because they understand that power comes in two forms: organized people and organized money. An effective broad-based collective is many organized institutions with some organized money in the form of dues. Judaism, Christianity, and Islam are examples of institutions that have survived for thousands of years because they understand how to organize people and money. Dues are the life blood of civil-society organizations because they create ownership and ensure a measure of independence in dealing with the powers that be. Goethe had it right: "Whosoever eats my bread, sings my song." A solid dues base will open the doors of power because heavy hitters in the state and market will recognize and deal seriously with the leaders of independent, financially self-sustaining efforts.

Dues also matter because power precedes program. When a broad-based collective has a well-organized base of people and some money, it can deal with officials and corporations with integrity and dignity intact. "We pay our own way. We are not here to ask for money for our operations. Our operating budget is $X per year, and we raise that ourselves from our member institutions. We don't want your money to operate; we want your help to build low-income homes." Such financial freedom gives an organization the dignity and strength to ask, not beg, for what it wants.

Broad-based organizations are led and controlled by a frequently changing leadership collective, which is mentored by professional organizers who change regularly. The paid organizing staff is small, two or three at most, sometimes only one. The IAF organization is an instrumentality created, funded, and led by leaders from the same civil-society institutions whose money pays its bills.

The second mark of an IAF organization is the presence of a talented professional organizer who belongs to a real network and has a record that can be checked out. While most of the work of broad-based organizations rests on its volunteer leaders, professional organizers are a crucial catalyst. They must have track records, be compensated well in salary and fringe benefits, and held accountable by the leadership. Alinsky thought that after five or six years, organizations either disband or become part of the establishment. The presence of his organizers in a community then was understood to be temporary. An important insight of the modern IAF, however, is that as instruments of citizen democracy, broad-based organizations are as necessary to the functioning of modern societies as efficient markets and effective states. And a small staff of professionally trained, mentored, and supervised organizers is necessary to the health of these organizations. IAF's professional organizers are talent scouts, teachers, mentors, agitators, and strategists. Their vocation is both simple and profound: to challenge and support citizens and people of belief—democratic or religious—to claim their public selves, to develop their political clout, and to learn how to stand for the whole.

An organization that fudges on either dues or the professional organizer will end up as a subsidized civic effort or a flash-in-the-pan movement that appears briefly in the media and then disappears.

Two Broad-Based Power Organizations

Communities Organized for Public Service (now Metro COPS) is an organization of parishes and other congregations originally based in the predominantly Hispanic, low-income West and South Sides of San Antonio. Founded in 1974, it is the oldest of the modern IAF organizations in the IAF network. For nearly thirty years, COPS has brought hundreds of millions of dollars' worth of new streets, drainage, sidewalks, libraries, parks, and streetlights to poor neighborhoods. It has brought about the demolition of substandard housing and the building of new housing. It has directed economic development funds toward poor inner-city neighborhoods. It has created Project

Quest, one of the nation's most highly acclaimed workforce preparation programs.

Beyond rebuilding the physical infrastructure of formerly marginalized parts of the city, COPS has transformed the culture of San Antonio's public life. It has created a public space in which issues are discussed and debated in the open, which is fiercely nonpartisan, and which allows for competition among a plurality of interests. COPS is committed to neighborhood and family values, democratic participation, leadership development, and public accountability of local and state officials.

The organization nurtures leaders and future leaders, who rise through its ranks, developing their skills and teaching others what they have learned. COPS has taught its leaders how strength lies not in specific issues or personalities but in the process of empowerment and leadership development. In this process, COPS continues to initiate in the process of rebuilding the city. Some of its successes include

- formulating the plan for a $10 million housing trust fund to finance affordable housing in inner-city neighborhoods
- organizing the San Antonio Education Partnership to guarantee job and scholarship opportunities to high school seniors from poor neighborhoods
- leadership in the creation of Project Quest, a nationally recognized comprehensive job training and placement effort
- negotiating and supporting a $140 million bond issue to provide continued street and drainage improvements
- blocking a proposal to sell the municipally owned electric utility to private interests, which would have resulted in significant increases in utility rates
- developing the Alliance Schools strategy for organizing to strengthen local public schools

Baltimoreans United for Leadership Development (BUILD) is a metropolitan, broad-based, multidenominational, nonpartisan organization that represents the strength and concerns of Baltimore's families through its churches. Its track record includes the following:

- a successful campaign against bank redlining that led to negotiated agreements with Baltimore banks and savings and loans, resulting in more than 500 low-income families acquiring home mortgages

- an agreement with the mayor, the corporate community, the school system, and sixteen area colleges and universities that guarantees financial
  aid for advanced education or a job to any student graduating from high
  school with a Maryland diploma and good attendance
- a campaign to raise the minimum wage paid to city workers and the
  employees of city contractors
- a pioneering effort to organize temporary workers

More than sixty broad-based citizens organizations like Metro COPS and
BUILD make up the national IAF network. Each of them stands for the whole
where they are, by winning on issues like those listed above. Because these
organizations understand that power precedes program, their work begins
with hundreds of thousands of relational meetings. Issues arise from there.
One of the toughest things to teach a new organization is to build its power
base before it goes into action. In the process of planning, acting, and evaluating on issues like these, such organizations do more than get streets repaired,
schools built, people insured, seniors protected, and homes built. They re-
weave the social fabric of a community across the lines of race, religion, geog-
raphy, and class. They generate the social capital that makes life not only
livable, but meaningful.

Creating Social Capital

Academics and pundits love to throw around the term "social capital" and
debate its nuances, but most of them couldn't organize a block party. IAF's
broad-based organizations are powerful social-capital generators.

The great driving force in today's world is unfettered capitalism. Marx
captured the dynamic driving force that turns money into capital in his famous general formula for capital, M—C—M′, in which M is money, C is a
commodity to be sold, and M′ is more money.[7] In that equation, profit =
M′−M. Capital grows only when the M—C—M′ process is in constant motion, creating more profit. Capitalism is not about money, which is merely a
means to an end; it's about keeping money in motion, the activity that generates profit. The more constantly and efficiently the M—C—M′ cycle can be
kept in motion, the more capital can be generated. For example, in today's
economy, nearly $2 trillion changes hands daily in the international currency
exchange market. The more constantly and efficiently the M—C—M′ cycle
can be kept in motion, the more capital can be generated.

The social (or political) capital of a citizens organization is its power to
win on its interests. That power is rooted in the meanings, values, social

knowledge, and relationships that hold such groups together in a community of common interests. Social capital is the shared "wealth" of the body politic. By analogy to Marx, its formula might be expressed as: TEP—CA—TEP', in which TEP is talent, energy, and power; CA is collective action; and TEP' is more talent, energy, and power. Kept in motion, organized talent, energy, and power generates social capital.

The social capital of a broad-based organization grows only when the organization is in action. Every relational meeting, house meeting, research action, and small or large public event leads to TEP'. Broad-based organizing is a process for creating social capital and keeping it in motion. Creating significant social capital requires organizing people on a size and scale that permits them to initiate action (motion), rather than merely reacting to the pressure of others. Single-issue organizations cannot sustain large amounts of social capital and keep it in motion week in and week out. Broad-based citizens organizations are powerful instruments for the generation of social capital because its citizens are organized—in place and in position, ready to act with purpose when called upon.

The creation of civil-society capital is one moment in the continuously dynamic existence of people and their institutions, a moment that transforms their power to act on behalf of their interests. It does not involve physical, material objects in any essential way. Nothing is bought or sold. It is not tangible, for it is embodied in relations among persons and their institutions, already existing ones and the new ones they are creating by acting. Social capital can't be preserved like jelly; you use it or you lose it. People grow, learn, and change inside this dynamic of collective planning, action, and reflection. When, and only when, people participate in the collective creation of social capital, their politicalness is expanded. Otherwise, it remains an unrealized potential, a failure to exercise the gift our Creator gave us. Creating social capital is an ongoing, unending task for those committed to act for justice and democracy. Religious organizations call this public work mission and ministry. Citizens institutions call it common good and meaningful public life.

The Vocation of Politicalness

Human beings are creatures of flesh and blood. Meaning comes only when they put that flesh and blood in the service of a larger purpose. People's talent, energy, and power *will* serve some purpose; the meaning and satisfaction they experience depends on whether they're serving goals worthy of their lives. If the purposes to which they devote their time and energy are worthy (for example, democracy, justice, love), people will flourish; if not (for example, crass materialism or self-preoccupation), people will be prone to addiction, nihilism, and despair. The question is not whether human lives serve some purpose, but only which purposes they serve.

Sheldon Wolin explained politicalness this way: "By politicalness I mean our capacity for developing into beings who know and value what it means to participate in and be responsible for the care and improvement of our common and collective life."[8] That one needs a little unpacking. Politicalness is a *capacity*. That means that it may, but will not automatically, be developed. Being able to act well politically is like being able to sing a song or give a speech; it's an ability that remains dormant if not practiced. Developing our politicalness requires that we know and value what it means to have power, and that means developing the head, the heart, and the gut. Exercising politicalness demands that we participate in something larger than our individual projects, and that means give-and-take, compromise, and mutual respect. Being political entails responsibility. Rabbi Abraham Heschel boiled the message of the Jewish prophets down to this: "Few are guilty, but all are responsible."[9] Our politicalness is our God-given ability to respond to our world as it is by joining with others to stand for the whole.

Our politicalness is a lot like our sexuality. We get it at birth and we have it all our lives. The capacity to be able, to have effects, on our world is as much a part of us as the capacity to form bonds of affinity with others. Politicalness and sexuality are ingrained in us, but neither of them is absolutely clear. Bernard Crick puts the point this way:

> [Politics and sexuality] are both activities in which . . . the sympathies that are a product of experience are better than doctrines that are learnt from books. Sexuality, granted, is a more widespread activity than politics, but again the suspicion remains that the man who can live without either is either acting the beast or aping the god. Both have much the same character of necessity in essence and unpredictability in form. Both are activities that must be carried on if the community is to perpetuate itself at all, both serve this wider purpose, and yet both can become enjoyable ends in themselves for any one individual . . . .[10]

So we're back again to social knowledge. Politics and sexuality are complex, ambiguous activities in which people regularly do the right things for the wrong reasons, and vice versa. As with our sexuality, there is no one right way to develop our God-given capacity for politicalness into an ability and a vocation. You have to grow into being a citizen just as you have to grow into being a sexual partner. It's like a kid learning a sport—you don't do it without practice. IAF organizations are the instruments that let people practice and evaluate public life in collectives. Through that activity they become founding fathers and mothers in their own right in their communities. IAF broad-based organizing constantly challenges those who are doing the relational meetings and public actions to change, to become citizens.

The problem is that average Americans don't see politicalness as a vocation or have a clue about how to develop that piece of themselves. Nor do they have a vehicle for figuring it out. We have a context for developing our sexuality. It's called family and private life. But where do we learn to develop our politicalness? The fact that so few Americans could answer that question means that most of them couldn't organize change in their communities if their lives depended on it. The thing is, they do.

Living out our religious and democratic values requires that public life be part of our citizenship and mission. Our politicalness has to be something we work at, interact with others about, and keep centered in and around the issues and values that we feel are important. People who understood the vocation of politics built this country. That's how hospitals and colleges and universities were started by religious institutions. That's how the local city Democratic Party got started, by building on the fabric of parishes and congregations that were already organized. If social efforts aren't constantly organized and if people don't see that they have an ongoing mission and vocation to participate in public life, to be a neighbor, to enter into arrangements of power with people across racial, religious, and class lines, and to welcome the differences, politics dies.

IAF leaders and organizers understand from their own experience what the sociologist Max Weber meant when he described politics as being like "the long, slow boring of hard boards," an activity not for the faint-hearted or those whose attention and gratification span is limited to "now." In a famous passage stressing the real demands of the world as it is, Weber's verdict on "movement" politics, on those who exercise their politicalness haphazardly or only when they feel like it, is sobering: "They have not measured up to the world as it really is in its everyday routine. Objectively and actually, they have not experienced the vocation for politics in its deepest meaning, which they thought they had."[11] Broad-based organizing is the most potent form now available for the development of our political birthright, for taking up our political vocation. We must grab politicalness by its roots.

4

Relationships: Private and Public

"The more realistically one construes self-interest, the more one is involved in relationships with others. . . . The more one is involved in relationships with others, the more conflicts of interest, or of character and circumstance, will arise."

BERNARD CRICK

Relationships: Private and Public

In the IAF organizing tradition, the foundational concept is relationship. In this chapter, I'll distinguish two basic types, private relationships and public ones. The distinction between the private and public domains is important, in fact crucial, and I contrast them here for purposes of understanding. In the world as it is, people are more or less in one mode or the other most of the time. Real understanding of private and public relationships comes from reflecting on experience.

The privateness/publicness of human life is both/and, not either/or. We are made this way by the Creator through our parents. In the previous chapter, I said that human beings are born with creative capacities called sexuality and politicalness. Sexuality is at the core of our being and relationships. It is the innate, wired-in instinct to be related to others in bonds of affinity. Our sexuality is part and parcel of all that we do and all that we are, but intimate sexual self-expression is only appropriate in the private realm of relationships. Cultures differ in the kinds and degree of sexual expression considered appropriate in public, but too much publicness in the expression of sexuality universally signals a problem of some kind.

Politicalness is also part of all that we are and do, but it is in the quintessentially public realm of life. Standing for the whole—engaging in strong debate, reasoned compromise, and focused action for the common good—requires that we participate in the public domain. When human politicalness is relegated to private relationships, which is one of the main effects of the dominant culture of individualism, it is distorted into narrow, private, ego-driven struggles. Private life is too small a stage for developing our political capacity.

Public and private are always in tension inside our skins. The trick is to learn not to mix them inappropriately—there are limits and boundaries. That learning comes hard in a culture where a multibillion-dollar advertising juggernaut deliberately and constantly mixes them up by stealing images from the private realm ("Reach out and touch someone," "Home for the holidays") and using them to sell stuff in the public marketplace. Co-opting sacred private realities like the bond between husband and wife or the shape of your body for the purpose of selling products is a hallmark of unbridled capitalism.

Private relationships are foundational and inform all others. They are personal, unique, intimate, and many times secret. The small circle of private relationships typically includes self, spouse, children, extended family, and a very few close friends. When these relationships are supportive and nurturing, they feed and sustain us throughout our lives; when they are not, they continue to undermine us. The sixteen to eighteen years at the beginning of our lives should be invested in forming us. The key institution in the realm of private relationships is the family.

The glue of the private domain is self-giving love. In this mode, we are bound by commitments, as well as by blood and genes, to understand and support one another until death do us part. The relationship between a mother and son or a father and daughter is unique and not duplicable. This is where we first learn reciprocity and self-sacrifice, mutual obedience and fidelity, where we gather the formative social knowledge of what it means to be in a relationship. It is our basic training ground in love and power, and here the love mode is stronger. Private relationships are covenants, unconditional promises of mutual commitment.

Public relationships, by contrast, are open, formal, capable of withstanding scrutiny, above board, and accessible to all. The glue of public relationships is also different. Here the ground rule is *quid pro quo*—you help me, I'll help you. This is where we learn about making and keeping public promises, and about how to hold and be held accountable. Enlightened self-interest, not mutual self-sacrifice, is what makes public relationships work. Here the power mode is stronger than the love mode. This is the world of exchange, compromise, and deals—the world of contracts, transactions, and the law.

Everybody wants and needs to be liked. It is an essential form of recognition, but it belongs primarily in the private realm, at home, where people are among those who take them for who they are. But this need does have a counterpart in public relationships. When people move toward powerful individuals in public life, they tend to want to be liked by them, but when that desire plays too large a role in their public actions, their integrity and power will be compromised.

Three thousand members of IAF's East Los Angeles Organization waited to pin the mayor, to hold him accountable. Mrs. Margarita Rodriguez, a Hispanic leader, introduced him, saying, "I present to you the mayor of Los Angeles, the Honorable Thomas Bradley." Bradley took the podium and said, "Thank you, Margarita." She spun in her tracks and returned to the microphone. "It's Mrs. Rodriguez to you today, Mr. Mayor." The mayor apologized.

By acting publicly in order to be liked, people invariably violate their group or organization's self-interest, usually by failing to hold public power-brokers accountable at critical moments. Margarita Rodriguez followed her instincts, making the distinction between private and public clear to the mayor and the members of her constituency.

What people need in public life is to be respected, which is similar to, but different from, being liked. That is why it is crucial to learn to act for respect in public, to be disinterested about being liked there, to look for liking in the private realm. Effective action sometimes brings both respect and liking, but the first is what matters in the public realm. The most recent in the continuing series of public figures who got liking and respect mixed up inappropriately was Bill Clinton, who thought he could mix public and private with impunity, be President and just plain Bill. He will not be the last. Prophets, visionaries, and ordinary people who value justice and democracy can't be too concerned about being liked in the public realm, but they must insist upon being respected there.

In the private mode, self-giving love is the centerpiece. This is where social bonding happens first and most intensely, generating trust, loyalty, and mutual obligation. Mutual fidelity and obedience are part of the practical chemistry of private relationships. Private life is largely about responding to the personal needs of those involved. To expect these nurturing ideals in public relationships is misleading and misguided. In the public mode, the ability to act—to be able—is the fulcrum of how social change happens and self-interest is realized. The dynamic is give and take. Public relationships involve the exercise of power, *quid pro quo*. They are not about unconditional private loyalties but rather about making and keeping public promises, initiating, compromising, and accountability.

The leaders of the new East Brooklyn organization were impatient and challenged the organizers: "We've been meeting for more than a year. When are we going to do something about all this blighted property?" The organizers knew that the organization was too young and not powerful enough to take on an issue of that size. Mike Gecan and I sweated to come up with a feasible alternative. I mentioned to him how hard the absence of street signs made it to find my way around when I came into the neighborhood. He said, "It's like that all over here." The absence of street signs gave the police and fire departments an excuse for not coming into the neighborhood. We started a three-month campaign involving several actions with the borough president of Brooklyn to get street signs replaced. They appeared three months after our last action, a wonderful symbol of new beginnings in East Brooklyn. That beginning led to improved grocery stores, thousands of Nehemiah homes, and community-controlled schools and a medical clinic.

This is the kind of compromise that public relationships require. Nobody gets exactly what they want when they want it, but everyone gets something in their interest.

The immutable "law of change" that I covered in Chapter One operates in both the private and public arenas. In the private domain, people long for peace, harmony, and certainty. If they are lucky and determined, they get a taste of unity, stability, and mutual understanding over time with family and friends. They learn to let down their guard and "just be." They drop their masks. When private life works well, the law of change means that moments of tension are resolved fairly in a climate of mutual trust.

In the public world, by contrast, people must be disciplined, alert, on guard, and conscious of what *persona* they must bear, what behavior is appropriate to the role they are representing. Public life demands calculation, weighing the possibilities and costs, the risks and benefits, associated with available choices. It's what the business world and work world are all about. Here the law of change means struggle, conflict, and controversy, punctuated only briefly with fleeting flashes of God's mercy and justice appearing, here and now. Once again, there is no easy way to get change in the public realm.

In the private world, choice is severely limited. Nobody asked you if you wanted to be thrown at birth into a particular history, culture, politics, and economics, and no one consulted you about who your parents, siblings, and extended family would be. People are born into particular, concrete, diverse, ambiguous circumstances and must play the hand they have been dealt. Like Job, they can bemoan the struggle, but at the end of the day they must cope with what they got.

To act on self-interest is required for self-development, and enlightened self-interest allows a self to emerge fully. Self needs other. Contrary to the dogma of privatized individualism, greater freedom is available in the public realm than in the private. Moving beyond the narrow limits of family, ethnic clan, and class means having more opportunities for relationships, jobs, education, ownership, etc., than can ever be realized in private or only with others like us. If you can celebrate only your own ethnic and religious heritage, you'll mix poorly in public relationships or not at all. This mixing of differences, energy, time, talent, and sweat is exactly what broad-based organizing is about. Embracing plurality—deliberately cultivating a blend of beliefs, ethnicity, and class—brings public strength to a collective like nothing else can. Strong broad-based organizations always move toward inclusion, striving to look like the larger constituencies they stand for. When they succeed, they take the "divide and conquer" strategy away from power brokers.

Human power and freedom only expand when people develop their politicalness within a large, diverse collective in public life. Inside public collectives, people insist upon and can hold multiple loyalties, some in conflict with one another, as the following story makes clear.

One Saturday morning, a man who had been active in the Organization of the Southwest Side approached me in our office there. He said, "Ed, I believe in what you're doing here; that's why I've been involved. But I need you to know that I'm not just a police officer, I'm on the red squad. We've been watching you closely for the past three months." That explained the fact that the glove compartment of my car and my apartment had been rifled several times in the past six months. I thanked him for telling me. He stayed in the organization, and neither of us ever said anything to the other leaders. I began to understand that public life is messy, and loyalties are divided.

Like this leader, all of us are both/and, more or less, as is/should be.

Democratic freedom is always relative, a matter of more or less. While the opportunity to claim a public life is critical for everybody, it's an especially strong antidote to the historical sexism that limits women's participation to the realm of private relationships and the institutionalized racism that relegates nonwhites to the sidelines of power arrangements.

The distinction between private and public sheds light on many things, including the state of synagogues, churches, and mosques today. There is a communal dimension to religious institutions, a necessary concern about personal acceptance and belonging (often called fellowship). The holy books make plain that churches, synagogues, and mosques are called to the public mission of changing the world. Today, however, religious institutions often cave in to the dominant culture's privatizing pressures and become havens for individuals seeking respite from the pressures and stresses of life. Today's mega-churches have a new golden rule: "Don't make any demands on people." They make people welcome. They make them comfortable. They find out what their needs are and service them. They support those who come, but don't challenge them. In other words, they violate Alinsky's Iron Rule by doing for others what they could and should be doing for themselves.

This surrender to individualism privatizes institutions that are called by their own sacred teachings to be a strong public presence. Religious institutions down through the ages have too often dichotomized private and public and then treated the private as sacred while dismissing the public as profane. When it takes hold of people's imaginations, this division of private and public into sacred and secular undermines the power of religion's publicness. Another version of this privatization occurs when secular materialists, who deny the reality of the spiritual dimension, preach and advertise the needs of number one as the be all and end all of existence.

There are habits and strengths of character that can only be learned and developed in private relationships, the virtues of self-sacrificing love. There are others that can only be learned and tested in the public arena, the virtues of enlightened self-interest. These complementary virtues are grounded in the development of our sexuality and politicalness, respectively. Unless both dimensions are integrated in our personalities, we are fragmented and disoriented. When we get public and private relationships mixed up, both suffer; when they are held in creative tension, both flourish.

Don't make the mistake of equating "private" with "personal." Both the private and public domains are personal, because what's personal is what we invest our hopes, passion, talent, time, and energy in. What we take personally is what we care about. Kept in the proper balance, and this is an ever shifting one, public and private relationships enrich each other. People who are fully alive invest themselves in private and public and know the difference.

In the culture of individualism today, people are largely deprived of the opportunity to develop public virtues, to exercise their political birthright. They are constantly pressured to obsess about private matters (my weight, my sex life, my promotion). Thus, the need is urgent for broad-based citizens organizations, where people can develop their politicalness. The people trained by IAF leave with an appetite for public life. They are willing to enter the public square and create a space where thought and meaning can be acted upon, and in that process they grow because there's a whole process of research, action, and reflection. In that process, they get social knowledge; they become powerful because social knowledge is deep and rich in values and thus trumps scientific knowledge, academic knowledge, and political knowledge. Informed citizens need that kind of knowledge to take on the received culture, of which we are all a part. The received culture must be challenged and changed.

Citizens see themselves as active, informed members of civil society. If they take citizenship as a vocation, then they do solve problems. And they operate inside the Iron Rule—they don't do things for people that people can do for themselves. They mobilize others with energy and talent like they have to go into action, and they're willing to pay dues to the organization that organizes that, so that no outside sources control it. They leverage their institutions to make that happen. It's the combination of leaders with their institutions that can move things politically. The challenge is how to move politically to realize some of the destiny you want for your family, your community, your city, your state, and your country. Electoral politics is the lowest form of participation. It's important, but without public life it's meaningless, because you don't get a say in who the candidates are. You've got to be a millionaire to run for the presidency or the senate of the United States.

Keeping Private and Public Straight

This analysis of two kinds of relationships comes down to one thing: understanding and respecting boundaries. As I said at the outset of this chapter, public and private are always in tension inside our skins; the trick is to learn not to mix them inappropriately—there are limits and boundaries. I want to be clear about which kinds of behavior are appropriate and necessary in relationships and why.

Clear thinking matters here, because IAF's experience has taught us that most of the difficulties that broad-based organizations have reflect problems in the private lives of their leaders and organizers. The distinctions between private and public have been developed and taught during IAF national training over the past thirty years, and sometimes people go back home and apply the training in unexpected ways, with interesting results.

An irate call from San Antonio came into the IAF national headquarters for "Mr. Chambers." When I got on the line, an angry voice said, "What are you teaching my wife in that training of yours? I didn't want her to go in the first place, and now she says she's not cooking every night unless some things change around here. What the hell are you guys you up to, anyway? I asked to speak with his wife. She said, "I'm doing an action on him, just like you taught us." I explained to her that actions were for the opposition, not your husband. "Oh," she said, "I'm very sorry. I'll only use what you taught me in public."

Many participants in national training come to see the public/private distinction as a treasure, a fruitful insight into what's working and not working in their lives. But their appreciation of the private/public distinction is often delayed, as if they can't let it in right away. My conclusion is that people's typical first reaction is actually twofold. First, clarity about public and private seems not only accurate but also important to them. Second, they are embarrassed or even ashamed to realize that they have been getting public and private mixed up. It takes a little time to integrate this.

As you reflect on these pages, if you find that you have been mixing up public and private, it's not your fault. You get no help from television, modern advertising, politicians, and even most religious leaders. Apart from IAF, formative institutions are not teaching and reflecting on what you have just read. Don't get discouraged. Just learn to ask yourself, "Where am I, more or less, right now, private or public?" Then act accordingly. Reflect on what happens as you get clearer, then teach the next generation.

5

The Practice of Public Life:
Research, Action, and Evaluation

"Great deeds are not done by strength or speed or physique, they
are the products of thought and character and judgment."

CICERO

Oxygen for the Body Politic

After Saul Alinsky's death, one commentator noted that part of his legacy was
a new twist on a familiar word in our vocabulary: an "action." "Action" is an
abstract word. It can never be understood in itself. Its conjugal partner is the
inevitable reaction. IAF defines an action as a public meeting of leaders of a
broad-based organization with political, business, or other officials for the
purpose of being recognized and getting them to act on specific proposals put
forward by the organization. Alinsky said, "Action is to the organization as
oxygen is to the body." The creative development of this public art form is
what the IAF network is justly famous for.

We call them actions, not meetings. We activate the dynamics of action
and inevitable reaction. Our organizers and leaders are sophisticated enough
about politics to know that you won't get what you want now, but you can
run a tactic or an action that gets you some of what you want next week. Our
strategies and actions are designed to get the powers that be to give and to
capitulate; that requires massive numbers of organized people aimed at the
right targets at the right times.

All real political action is aimed deliberately and is calculated and focused,
and our actions are that way. We play to win. That's one of the distinctive
features of IAF: We don't lead everyday, ordinary people into public failures,
and we're not building movements. Movements go in and out of existence.
As good as they are, you can't sustain them. Everyday people need incremen-
tal success over months and sometimes years. IAF organizations didn't get

power in the states of Texas and Maryland easily; it took us fifteen or twenty years.

When organized people claim some power, the usual power brokers have something new to contend with.

> New York City Mayor Ed Koch had persistently refused to meet with East Brooklyn Congregations' black and Hispanic leaders about building affordable housing in East New York. That changed when Bishop Mugavero of Brooklyn called for an appointment. The bishop, who understood the ways of power, volunteered to lead the EBC delegation to City Hall.
>
> Upon arrival, the small delegation was ushered into the private quarters of the Mayor and served coffee by women wearing white gloves. The servers seemed amazed at the presence of two black women in the delegation. When the meeting began, only the mayor and the bishop spoke. Their talk was formal for the first three minutes, with Koch calling Mugavero "Your Excellency." Suddenly, Bishop Mugavero changed gears. "Ed," he said, "my Protestant brethren and I have committed $12 million for this affordable housing program, and I need $10 million from the city. The money is needed for one-time grants of $10 thousand each to the first thousand homeowners." Koch spluttered and pleaded that the city's money was already committed. The bishop paused, looked him in the eye, pointed his finger across the small table between them, and said, "Ed, this is important. If necessary, steal it." After another pause he added, "And I'll forgive you."
>
> Ten days later on the steps of New York's City Hall, the bishop and the mayor officially announced the Nehemiah affordable housing program, to the cheers of thousands from East Brooklyn.

In describing Alinsky's law of change ("Change means movement; movement means friction; friction means heat; heat means controversy") in the first chapter, I said that all significant change comes about through a threat or pressure. The movement tactics of the 1950s and '60s are not relevant at the beginning of the twenty-first century, but you still can't get social change without confrontation, because the haves never give you anything real. If you're a have-not, they'll give you crumbs—they'll give you low-paying jobs, minimum-wage jobs if they can, when you're fighting for a living wage. They'll resist and fight you—like Koch.

Consensus is nice, but it belongs in the private realm. Unity, harmony, and good feelings happen with your friends and your kids and a few others.

But public life is about power, self-interest, and the ability to make change happen. There's no nice way to get change. Read the Book of Job. God is trying to teach Job about struggle, and Job is begging God to give him life. All life is an eternal struggle, and it's as much a struggle at seventy-five, as it is at fifty-five, or fifteen.

Practicing public life starts with people in their institutions, central-city people and suburbanites, where they are in the world as it is. We try to take people in that world of real needs and necessities and move them toward the world where they ought to be. That's an ongoing, tension-filled struggle with victories, learning experiences, and some failures. It's a process. John Dewey called democracy a way of life. Nice words, but what do they mean? In IAF that way of life involves a way of doing public actions invented and continually crafted over the last half-century as means of creating the pressure that leads to change. Without action, an organization is only a paper tiger or a bureaucracy.

IAF organizations understand that digested actions are worth more than a university degree because they result in social knowledge.

A hard campaign to unionize garment workers in Mississippi seemed to have resulted in success when a majority of workers at one plant voted to join the union. The celebration tuned into a funeral when the "victorious" workers reported the next day only to be informed by the manager that the plant was shut down. "Go home," he said. That same afternoon, a video crew recorded a bulldozer demolishing the building. When the now-discouraged labor organizer went fifty miles down the road to another plant, the workers greeted him with ridicule, telling him to move on. The company had shown the video at all its other plants in the state. Low-wage worker organizing in Mississippi was over.

Drawing on sixty years of experience, IAF organizations understand and teach what this story makes plain: "The action is in the inevitable reaction." An action is initiated to get a response, to start a negotiation process. That's why a good action is aimed at provoking specific responses from carefully chosen targets. "If elected, will you, Mr. or Ms. Candidate, meet with a delegation of our leaders during your first month in office to establish a deadline for installing pedestrian crosswalks at the three intersections we have identified this afternoon? Please answer yes or no. If you can't, we have a third category called wishy-washy." Pointed questions expecting answers aimed at officials with the power to respond start a public conversation.

In private life, we understand that it's important to get to specifics with family and friends when there's a problem. People inexperienced and untrained in public action tend not to initiate pointedly and strategically. They react. They protest. They vent their grievances, trying to catch attention that fuels some outrage and hoping that something constructive will come about. The movers and shakers who dominate public life, however, understand the shelf life of such events. They just wait for the public's attention to flit elsewhere. Do you ever see the same headline two days in a row?

> The local headline read, "Church and Civic Leaders Confront Legislators on Casino Vote." The story described several hundred community leaders boarding buses on the day of the final vote to stand on the steps of the state capitol to protest the legislature's likely passage of a bill allowing a land-based casino in New Orleans. Their numbers were impressive, their speeches forceful and eloquent. Political observers agreed that the outcome of the vote was not affected in the slightest by the protest. It was too little, too late. The land-based casino had become a money winner.

An effective action isn't activity for its own sake. It must be aimed, focused, and deliberate to provoke the inevitable reaction. In an action, your moral stance must be twofold; one side obviously is your position, but even more important is what you do to cause a reaction of recognition or rebuff. You must weigh both the action and the potential reaction. That's how real-world morality works. Kick-in-the-glass or burn-baby-burn activists and terrorists ridicule this real-world morality. Their answer is, "From the ashes a new phoenix will arise." Kamikaze types are amoral and antipolitical. Violence is antipolitical; it destroys politicalness.

The exercise of democracy requires a space where citizens can appear publicly, not as individuals acting on single interests, but representing collectives that do politics. This space for exercising politicalness is what a broad-based organization creates. Staying in the public dialectic of action/reaction over time with those who have serious political and economic clout requires organized people. People seek justice, and they may seek it right now, but their wiser political selves recognize the truth of Weber's classic description of politics as "a long, slow boring of hard boards." The work of justice is the work of people organized for the long haul.

Research

The public practice honed by the IAF over the past sixty years is "research, action, evaluation." Planning for an action begins with identifying targets in hundreds of relational and small-group meetings. The key word in the preceding sentence is "action." Actions are aimed toward something you can do something about. It's called an issue. Some things are so large as to overwhelm action efforts. These we term "problems," something you can do nothing about. The number of children living in poverty in America is a problem; training for single mothers with children is a possible issue for an organization with some power. The sale and consumption of illegal drugs is a problem; tearing down six specifically identified crack houses in a neighborhood is an issue. The dysfunction of urban public schools is a problem; getting rid of an abusive sixth-grade teacher is an issue. Effective actions target issues, not problems.

The research preceding an action begins with an internal power analysis. Do we have a winnable issue (not a problem) here? Do we have a sufficient number of leaders with followers who feel the issue is in their interest? Will they mobilize their supporters? Is it immediate enough? What are the turnout quotas for each group in order to win? Will the action build our organization? Answers to these questions will determine whether or not it is feasible and timely to proceed.

In preparing for an action, you must conduct an external power analysis of this issue. Who are the key decision-makers? Who will oppose us, and what is their relative strength? Who are our potential allies, and will they help on this? What allies must be talked to before we proceed? Who will our action upset and at what cost? Some of these questions can be answered by pooling the social knowledge of people in an organization. Others will require small, focused "research action" meetings with public officials and corporate power brokers. Remember: In organizing, there are no permanent allies and no permanent enemies.

Action

Read *Rules for Radicals* by Alinsky—especially his chapter on tactics.[1] He's right on target. When done right, an action is a public drama, like a play. Its basic plot has movement—personalizing and polarizing. In creating the plot for an action, "personalizing" means deliberately making someone the target of the attention of the group. Broad-based organizations understand better than most people that what's wrong is rarely one person's fault. The drama of an action, however, requires that a person—not a nameless, faceless bureaucracy like "city hall" or "the administration"—be put on the public hot seat, to be held accountable and urged to make a commitment to change something. It's not possible to confront the anonymous "system," which is an abstraction, and then hold it accountable for its response. That's why names and faces must be put to targets in plotting an effective action.

An action must not only personalize the issue but also polarize around it. Polarizing means creating public tension around an issue by confronting the target(s) with a large, diverse, disciplined crowd that plainly expects him or her to respond favorably to their proposals. Pointed questions to specific persons hang in the air during an action until answered by the target(s): Are you with us or against us on this issue? Polarizing means deliberately bringing the inevitable tension between change and harmony to the forefront. Of course, no situation is ever 100 percent one way or the other. Real life is more or less always ambiguous. Personalizing and polarizing are means to an end.

> A group of leaders from a New York City organization had been rebuffed repeatedly when they tried to get a meeting with their councilman to discuss an issue. So they took a delegation to his office and announced that they were waiting for him in the council meeting room and that a press conference would start in thirty minutes outside his door if he didn't show. When he appeared, the delegation members were sitting in the elevated chairs ordinarily reserved for the council. "So this is how you make your point," he said. They replied, "We've been going through channels for six weeks to get a meeting with you, our elected representative. You didn't even have the courtesy to return our calls. So why don't you take a seat down there for once, and get a taste of what city hall feels like to your constituents."

When personalized targets do 75 percent of the right thing (what we want), they're taken off the public hot seat by the citizens and receive an acknowledgment for their commitment. One classic way for this to happen in large meetings is through audience applause; another is for on-stage leaders to shake hands with the former targets. This is called depersonalizing and depolarizing, and it's critically important. Activists rarely do this. Ideologues never do it. Our cause is at best sixty-forty or seventy-thirty right. You could make an argument for the target's position. In electoral politics, fifty-one to forty-nine is a victory, but real-world democratic decision and action requires a much higher differential.

Among IAF affiliates, personalizing is not demonizing, and polarizing is not coercing. Like all powerful, nonviolent forms of political action, personalizing and polarizing create tension and make people uncomfortable. Like Gandhi's sit-down strikes and Martin Luther King's civil rights tactics, IAF actions have a way of afflicting the comfortable and comforting the afflicted.

It's as important politically to know how and when to relax the tension as it is to initiate and sustain it, when to depersonalize and depolarize.

The moral standard by which IAF leaders and organizers judge an action is not middle-class politeness. Rather, they must use their collective political judgment to calculate the reaction—the likely chain of effects that an action may produce. This requires social knowledge not only of the organization's interests but also of the interests of its allies and opponents. It means giving serious forethought to the likely responses of all three. It demands that an organization consider not only where things are likely to move around the issue for the action but also how other issues will be affected, as well as the effect on the organization's overall growth. This is the complex, real-world morality of using relational power.

Enacting such a public drama requires more than a plot. The stage must be appropriately arranged. Diverse roles must be assigned in a way that takes into account and stretches people's talents and limitations. The flow of events must be carefully crafted within a time frame of sixty to ninety minutes. Parts of the event must be rehearsed in advance like a play. The audience must be in place and disciplined. A floor team of leaders must keep on-stage leaders, invited officials, and the audience on task, and be prepared to improvise when necessary. Powerful actions start on time and end on time.

Evaluation

As a young boy growing up in Iowa, I loved to climb trees, especially if they were loaded with green apples. I also had a habit of falling out and breaking bones. That was in the Depression, when money for a doctor was a hardship. When I would slink in the back door holding my broken limb, my dear mother would berate me: "Edward, Edward, why don't you think before you climb?" The fact is that people act first and think afterward. Self-preservation demands that we defend everything we do and what we don't do. We defend our action with a rationale. When confronted with rationalizing, it's better to duck and weave and go on to something else.

Thinking and calculating go into preplanning an action, but not much thinking goes on during the action itself. We cannot think and act simultaneously. Try rubbing your belly and patting your head at the same time. Unless leaders draw off immediately after an action and evaluate it, little or no education takes place. During IAF's first thirty years, we didn't practice evaluation. Our action, both successful and failed, remained unprocessed. The art form of evaluation needs to happen immediately and on the spot. Talk to an orchestra director or a baseball batting instructor about how important timely feedback is. Movement activists don't believe in critical evaluation, and charismatic leaders avoid it, never allowing their charisma to be critiqued. Modern IAF lives and dies with the quality of our collectives' evaluations. Evaluations are our school of higher learning. No undigested happenings allowed.

Twenty people will hear and see the same event differently. These different feelings and takes have got to be voiced, discussed, and digested. This is where growth goes on and judgments are adjusted. The thirty or thirty-five minutes spent in evaluation are organizationally more important than the action. The action provides a common grist for reflection. The evaluation by the collective's leaders turns it into social knowledge. The same event is evaluated two weeks, two months, and sometimes two years later, providing ongoing food for learning and growth. A few years of taking part in high-quality evaluation is worthy of a B.A. degree in citizenship.

Several very large outdoor actions were held in the campaign to secure new Nehemiah homes for families in East Brooklyn. Immediately after one of them, which had brought out 4,000 people, forty-five leaders gathered for an evaluation. It went smoothly until a brave layperson said to the charismatic pastor who had rallied the troops, "This is the third time we've heard that same speech." Tough medicine for a key celebrity pastor. He sheepishly confessed, "I guess I will have to prepare for these events like I do for my sermons." Applause, growth, and the two men shaking hands afterward.

An effective evaluation begins with participants getting their feelings about the action out in one or two words. Then leaders analyze their behavior and the opposition's. Did the two sides recognize each other? Was there an exchange of power? What did we do well? What did we learn from them? How did you feel when our speaker told the mayor to shut up and listen? Did we have the right research? What do we do now? And on it goes for thirty to forty minutes.

Senior IAF organizer Arnie Graf recalls that as a young activist with the Congress on Racial Equality (CORE) in the 1960s, evaluation was simple: "Where's the next action?" Hearing this, Alinsky accused Graf of being a "pile of undigested happenings." Good, frank evaluation is IAF's tested antidote for undigested happenings. It generates social knowledge. And it keeps us from believing our own propaganda.

Recognition

A more fundamental concern underlies every issue on which organizations initiate an action. The need to be recognized as somebody and something is the deepest drive inside us. Infants work parents for recognition day and night. Young adults thrive on being noticed. The world of fashion feeds on the need to be recognized—white teeth, good hair, etc. Individuals, groups, and organizations develop in healthy ways only when their existence, identity, and importance are recognized and affirmed by others.

It was the early 1960s, and The Woodlawn Organization (TWO) was in a battle with the University of Chicago over a land grab south of the Midway. Many of the TWO residents had enough money to purchase a house after twice being removed by the city's slum clearance program. They and their relatives were facing the juggernaut of the University of Chicago and Major Richard J. Daley expanding the university's campus south by a mile. In the '50s, they had land-grabbed most of Hyde Park. The university's Law Department had been instrumental in drafting and enacting the hateful and un-American restrictive covenants for Hyde Park whites, keeping blacks out in the purchase of property.

On a hot Thursday night, 500 Woodlawn residents crowded into the church to plan for the showdown meeting with the mayor at city hall at 10:00 A.M. on Friday. Arthur Brazier was the elected leader and held forth on what awaited the mayor the next morning. Before the rally ended, he had the leaders on their feet cheering.

The large room on the fourth floor at city hall had 200 fixed seats, so TWO brought 205 residents, Reverend Brazier, and one white guy—me, the organizer. I stayed in the back row, a mistake. The mayor came in five minutes late, flanked by two policeman. Eight aides stood near the railing separating the black citizens from the mayor's team.

The strategy was to interrupt Daley, who always filibustered, after two minutes, get our demands on the table, and get out. You only had about fifteen or twenty minutes during these prearranged hearings. Reverend Brazier was glued to his seat for five minutes, ten minutes, and then finally as Daley was beginning to leave, Brazier demanded another meeting two weeks hence to consider and respond to his advice.

The 200 blacks from the previous night's rally had come to see their leader, Reverend Brazier, stand up to the powerful Irish mayor in this critical housing battle. When I got to the lobby with the four elevators, clusters of disappointed leaders were huddled in front of three of them.

Brazier was alone at the last elevator with his head down. I approached and asked if I could ride home with him instead of going on the buses.

As we headed south on Lake Shore Drive, he started: "I don't know what is wrong. I just can't interrupt the Mayor of Chicago." I said, "Reverend Brazier, last night you promised the troops you would." "I know," he said, "I just can't do it. Maybe I should quit." I had to change his thinking. From somewhere, I said, "Do you shower every morning?" "Why yes, certainly I do," he replied. I said, "You did one good thing today; you got us back there in two weeks. Now every morning for the next two weeks as you shower, you have a companion, Mayor Richard J. Daley. He's naked like you are, and he is soaping himself like you are, you got the idea? He puts his pants on one leg at a time, you know."

During the next twelve days, as Reverend Brazier strode into our headquarters, I rose from the back office and said "Good morning. How is our project coming?" He took a quick look to see if the secretaries were listening and then said, "Fine, Ed, fine."

Two weeks later, TWO was back at the fourth floor of city hall. This time, I was in the row directly behind Reverend Brazier. The plan was to strike on the mayor's first words: "Good morning." The mayor came in and stood near the podium with his white cops and white aides. On his "*Good* morning," Brazier sprang to his feet, leaned forward crossing the rail with hand and finger extended, coming within one foot of Daley's nose and shouted, "Mr. Mayor." Two cops went for the hips where their guns were. Daley drew back and blushed red, which he retained during the whole twenty-minute confrontation. Brazier got it all out in five minutes: "The injustice, the displacement again, we Negroes have rights too, etc. You can help resolve this, call a meeting between the university and TWO. Force a settlement." Flustered and beet red, without promising anything, Daley said he would see what he could do. The leaders cheered; Brazier was celebrated at the elevators. The folks saw public courage and felt recognized as they went back to their South Side homes.

The civil rights movement in Chicago was under way, because of a proud, dignified former mailman who knew his value and the value of his people.

Don't miss this point. In interaction, individually or in collectives, we crave the recognition of others. But people with some social knowledge of how power works understand that in the world as it is, recognition given can be taken away. In a working democracy, we must not only have the power to elect people but also to hold them accountable. That's what broad-based political collectives do.

Practice the trilogy: research, act, evaluate. But you can't do it alone. Serious action on public matters requires an organization, a diverse collective of people.

6

Reflections of an Organizer

"Our first intellectual obligation is to abandon the myth of stability that played so large a part in the modern age. . . . The future belongs not so much to the pure thinkers who are content—at best—with optimistic or pessimistic slogans; it is a province, rather, for reflective practitioners who are ready to act on their ideals. Warm hearts allied with cool heads seek a middle way between the extremes of abstract theory and personal impulse."

STEPHEN TOULMIN

As doctors are to patients, as lawyers are to clients, as coaches are to athletes, so are professional organizers to volunteer leaders in public life. In the United States, Tom Paine and Sam Adams come to mind as political organizers. In the arena of religion, Moses and Paul are classic examples of organizers. Organizers are not the center, but they place themselves at the center. Their focus is the human person, the holiest work of creation, embodied in family, congregation, and workplace. In IAF organizing, we birth and parent public life and public relationships. Organizing in the IAF network is a distinct and valued profession, a vocation. The kind of organizer I'll describe here has been trained and developed in the broad-based organizing approach of the IAF over the past thirty years.

An Organizer's Journey

I was raised in rural Iowa in the 1930s and '40s. I thought life came down to family and Roman Catholicism. Midwestern Iowa was hardly the center of the universe. For us five kids, contact with the outside world was sitting on the living room floor and listening to Father Coughlin's raves and FDR's fireside radio chats. There was no preparation in those days for a role in public life. (There still isn't.) The only three career possibilities ever mentioned to me were priest, lawyer, or schoolteacher, with priest heavily pushed.

After high school, I signed up to become a priest, enrolling at St. John's University, the Benedictine college at Collegeville, Minnesota. St. John's Abbey was the Benedictine center of the Roman Catholic liturgical movement in the 1940s and '50s. After my sophomore year, I split from academia and basketball to wander Europe for a year. I was after meaning and looking for roots. My father never wanted to go home to the village ten miles outside of Castlebar, County Mayo, to the Irish shed among the peat bogs, incest, a pig in the parlor, and no outhouse. He was the thirteenth child; his mother died in childbirth with number fourteen. I didn't realize it at age nineteen, but I was searching for less theory and more real people doing something about the world as it is.

My year of bumming around war-torn Europe turned out to be worth more than four years of college and one more of so-called theology in Latin. I encountered the French priest-worker movement, liturgical pioneer Pius Parsch, and theologian Henri de Lubac. I attended the *agape* mass behind Russian lines outside Vienna. What I saw in the Young Christian Student and Worker organizations planted seeds for a different life in the U.S. for me. I was radicalized by Europe's progressive Catholic leaders.

After finishing college at St. John's and the first year of theology in the diocesan seminary in Dubuque, Iowa, I began questioning the way things were done out of my experiences in Europe. Why not do the liturgy in English and turn the altar around to face the people of God? Once or sometimes twice a week, I was thrown out of the Latin-speaking theology classes for using English and for raising the issue of the priesthood of the laity.

Over the Christmas holidays, I asked for a meeting with my bishop in Sioux City, Iowa. Borrowing my dad's car, I traveled the 180 miles to get a hearing, seek advice, and hopefully receive some clarity on what priesthood was all about. I was twenty-three years old. In the ninety-minute meeting, Bishop Mueller was kind enough and heard my complaints. There were tears in both our eyes when, without turning around, he reached above his head and took the crucifix off the wall, turned it around, and said: "Mr. Chambers, you must obey and climb up here." A thunderbolt struck. So that's what it's about. A sad ride home followed. This romantic idealist was beginning his education into the world as it is.

You don't realize the force of power until it's used against you. My awakening came a few months later, when I was waiting in line with my classmates in the outer chapel for the 8:00 P.M. tonsure liturgy to begin. I had completed first theology, and tonsure was the first ritual step toward priesthood. A snippet of hair was cut from your head, symbolizing your admission into the clerical state. As I waited in line with my surplice over my arm, I was tapped on the shoulder by the rector of the seminary, who said, "Your bishop wants to talk with you." When we were in the room, the bishop overpowered me in six minutes. "We've been meeting all day about you," he said. "You ask too many questions. You hold cell meetings during recreation time to read French theologians. You talk about the priesthood of the laity. We are not going to tonsure you." I had one question for the bishop: "Why did you wait until the last moment?" From the last pew in the back, I watched thirty-five of my classmates receive tonsure, my first vision of failure.

After that, I hitchhiked from Iowa to New York City to Dorothy Day's Catholic Worker House. I was broke and hungry after four days on the road, and I found shelter at Friendship House, a Catholic interracial commune operating in Harlem in the 1950s. They had a storefront service center on Lenox Avenue and 134th St. That's how I stumbled into public life. What a school Harlem was in those days: slum lords, power brokers like Robert Moses, as well as Adam Clayton Powell, Murray Kempton, Sugar Ray Robinson, Dorothy Day, and Friendship House. I had Saul Alinsky's book and hundreds of everyday, ordinary people who taught me how to operate in public life. One of those lessons came the day Eamon Hennessey, a well-known anarchist buddy of Dorothy Day, and I were selling copies of *The Catholic Worker* newspaper for a penny apiece on opposite corners of Wall Street. Hennessey was arguing with guys in business suits while I was selling papers. After four hours, I had about 375 pennies, and he had twelve. "Here, Ed," he said, "give me the money and carry these extra papers. I'll turn it in to Dorothy." Back at Friendship House, he walked into Dorothy's office proudly proclaiming a good day's work. She looked over his shoulder and nodded at me. She knew who had sold the papers. A lesson for me on how the real world works.

I got lots of social knowledge, gained experientially. I lost my romantic idealism and began my entry into the real world of power struggles, conflict, and ambiguity. While I was on duty at Friendship House in the evenings, I noticed individuals and groups of people going down the back stairs to the cellar of our building. Curiosity got the best of me, and one evening at about 10 P.M. I went down the stairs. The black janitor in charge of the boiler gave me a sociology lesson. For a quarter you could sleep on the floor next to the furnace; other slots were a dime each. Thirty-five to forty people—men, women, and children—filled the damp, smelly basement floor. My idealism suffered another shock. Welcome to the world of the poor and hungry. I couldn't believe that humans had to live like that.

Two more years of Harlem slum living got me off the world as it should be and radicalized me to the world as is. I began to grasp experientially what

I would later find articulated by Saul Alinsky—meaning is somewhere in the tension between the two worlds.

During the 1950s, President Truman and the U.S. war machine also advanced my understanding of power, when I applied for conscientious objector status during the Korean War. Rough treatment, including a psychiatric evaluation and pressure to sign a loyalty oath, were all part of the deal. Only one sister from my family of seven siblings supported me. When the Webster County, Iowa, draft board discovered a Roman Catholic conscientious objector in their jurisdiction, they called me in, and then they called my former pastor, Father P. J. Sweeney, an ex-Marine Corps chaplain in World War II. His response—"Chambers, yeah, I know him. If you've got your hands on the s.o.b., lock him up"—didn't help much. The board stood by my 1A classification. I won by thirty days, when I turned twenty-six and automatically dropped out of the draft. Welcome to public life. I missed five years at hard labor in Fort Leavenworth, Kansas.

My move from do-goodism to organizing took about five weeks. Handing out old clothes at Friendship House on Tuesday and Thursday nights helped wise me up. One guy showed up every week, complaining, "They stole my shoes." One night after this had become a routine, I had my do-good assistant take over while I followed the guy with the new shoes I'd just given him. After turning the corner on Lenox Avenue, he ducked into the first hallway, promptly whipped off his shoes and gave them to a guy who handed him a bottle of Sneaky Pete—cheap wine. This is hardly interracial justice.

From Doing Good to FIGHT

Mr. Friendship, as the residents called me, had tried do-goodism in Harlem. Then I got into organizing. I started by building some no heat/no hot water tenants associations mainly with black mothers with kids. We would troop into court but have no way of talking to the judge about the injustices the slumlords were perpetrating on these women and their children. After a couple of frustrating efforts, I realized that with six black women and one white guy, the public setup required that I take the role of lawyer for the ladies. I raided the used clothing handout operation at Friendship House, put on a tie and a jacket, and walked into the judge's courtroom followed by the ladies. I said, "Your honor, these are the tenants of a building with no heat and no hot water. The ladies will give you thermometer readings taken in their apartments at 6:00 A.M. and 6:00 P.M. for the last three weeks." Then I quickly faded back behind them. We worked this public game for about five months and started winning against the landlords, until I got nailed for impersonating a lawyer. The threat of contempt charges sat me down in the front row, behind the rail of the legal sanctuary. In the meantime, developer Robert Moses came along with his bulldozer version of urban renewal and tore down the buildings faster than I could organize their tenants. I thought I was building power by organizing marginalized residents; I came to understand later that you've got to organize everybody.

At age twenty-six I began organizing for Saul Alinsky with the Citizens Foundation for Lackawanna in a suburb of Buffalo, New York. Nick von Hoffman had found out about my Harlem work and talked Saul into hiring me. On the founding day of the new organization, I was leading a protest in one of the poor wards near the Bethlehem Steel Plant, and the crowd started getting out of control. Some leftists were trying to take over the event, so I jumped on top of a car to take charge and restore order. It worked. The action ended peacefully. Later, this strange priest came up to me and said, "That was a nice job, kid." It was Father Jack Egan of Chicago, who had come to Buffalo for the founding event and to meet with Alinsky and Monsignor John J. O'Grady, the founder of Catholic Charities. I asked him where Alinsky and O'Grady were. He replied, "Back at the hotel having cocktails. You did a nice job today—good work!" Egan repeated as he waved goodbye. His words were important recognition for a young organizer learning by the seat of his pants. More than forty years later, I returned the recognition at Egan's funeral.

During the black power and civil rights movements of the mid-'60s, Alinsky assigned me to build a black power organization in Rochester, New York. A group of church liberals had contacted Alinsky and raised the money for an organizing drive after a 1964 riot exploded in Rochester's black ghetto, scaring the hell out of the white establishment. The television news bulletin on the night of the riot began: "It couldn't happen here in Rochester . . . but it did." Our fledging organization, called FIGHT (Freedom, Integrity, God, Honor, Today), was trying to build a relationship with the haves of Rochester, the Eastman Kodak Company. Our strategy was to start by negotiating a small arrangement with the then-progressive Xerox Company, which had allowed a union in its operation. Kodak had no unions and no relationship with the black community. As Alinsky put it, "Rochester, New York, is a Southern plantation transplanted north." We got our first breakthrough when the top executives of Xerox, including the president, agreed to a meeting to discuss the employment of six hardcore unemployed from the black community.

Five black Pentecostal and Baptist pastors, briefed and nervous, and I went to Xerox for the 2:00 P.M. meeting. Our leader and spokesperson was Minister Franklyn Florence, a protégé of Malcolm X, who had agreed to join FIGHT because Malcolm told him that Alinsky knew more about organizing than anybody. As we entered the corporate boardroom, the Xerox officials stood and extended their hands for a handshake. These two groups had never met or even seen each other before. Minister Florence rudely walked past all five outstretched hands, and the others with him followed suit. I slunk in, livid with anger. Needless to say, the so-called meeting was a dud. After about twenty minutes it was over. I clammed up on the elevator on our way down to the lobby. Then I found a corner and unloaded on Florence. I used strong, nonchurch language with my group of ministers. The other five judiciously affirmed my analysis of how not to get a relationship. Those kinds of mistakes were never made with powerful Kodak. Everybody learned, and a year later we had our six hardcore unemployed blacks working at Xerox, and then we took the fight to Kodak.

After weeks of secret negotiations, an Eastman Kodak vice president signed an agreement to bring 600 hardcore unemployed blacks into the all-white Kodak workforce of about 40,000. Because Kodak owned and dominated the community, the agreement made the front page of *The New York Times* the next day. But two days later, the announcer on the 10 o'clock news tore up the so-called FIGHT-Kodak pact on live television. It was two days before Christmas. At a Christmas party for black pastors that felt more like a wake, Minister Florence cornered me and said, "Ed, you would not believe the despair in the black community right now. You lied to me. You told me that we could trust Kodak, but you can't trust whites. The agreement was just a trick." He threatened to resign. After a huge rally in Rochester by the FIGHT organization against the Eastman Kodak Company for tearing up the signed agreement, a ringing phone roused me from a dead sleep at about 3:30 A.M. "Have you got Carmichael there? We're going to kill him and you." Stunned, I replied instinctively, "He's not here; he's at the fire station." Then I hung up. We got Stokley Carmichael, Mr. Black Power, who was actually sleeping at Minister Florence's home, safely out of town five hours later on the first plane.

After three weeks of despair, the FIGHT leadership and I dreamed up a shareholder tactic. We would purchase ten shares of Kodak stock in January and go to the annual shareholders meeting in April to protest their backing out of the signed agreement. Kodak's annual meeting was always held in Flemington, New Jersey, hundreds of miles from Rochester. We decided to get 1,000 members of black congregations at the meeting by busing them overnight to Flemington. The buses were scheduled to arrive between 6:30 and 7:00 A.M. Since they were going to spend ten hours on an overnight bus ride, the folks would need bathroom facilities, a cup of coffee, and maybe a sweet roll. Why not call upon our natural allies, the church folks of Flemington, population 3,500? We got a wonderful response from the mainline Catholic and Protestant churches, which agreed to receive 150 to 200 people at each of their facilities early on the morning we were scheduled to arrive. That changed a week before meeting. One by one, the Christian congregations of Flemington called, turning their backs on their brothers and sisters in Rochester over an issue of justice. Kodak had gotten wind of the strategy and went to work on Flemington's church leaders. Three thousand National Guard troops were called out on the day of the annual meeting, enough to give virtually every citizen of Flemington a personal bodyguard with a gun.

FIGHT was desperate two days before the Kodak event. We were down to one Missouri Synod Lutheran church that was still signed up to receive their share of our people, when a call came into our Rochester headquarters from its pastor. "I'm in trouble," he said. "My church board has called a special meeting tonight to decide whether I'm still the pastor." Minister Florence, FIGHT's president, pleaded with him to hold firm, since all our folks would need bathroom facilities. He agreed to call us after the meeting. A group of us waited at the headquarters for the pastor's call. When it came, all he said was: "I won eight to seven. Come on. We'll receive you."

We arrived in Flemington at 7:00 A.M. on the morning of the stockholders meeting in 32 buses, a totally nonviolent, disciplined, orderly group of over 1,000 black congregation folks coming to protest at Kodak's annual meeting, a first against an American corporation. Since we had to keep the group busy until the meeting began at 10:00, after our stop at the church we marched to the main headquarters of Kodak in the village and posted a copy of the signed agreement on their door. When the stockholders meeting began, our church folks remained outside, while Minister Florence, with nine other leaders, Saul Alinsky, and me, marched into the meeting of assembled stockholders as shareholders. After three minutes, Minister Florence took the floor microphone and interrupted the agenda: "Mr. Chairman, Mr. Chairman, will Kodak honor the agreement it signed with FIGHT?" The chairman replied, "No." Minister Florence announced that Kodak had one hour to reconsider. Then we turned and walked out with national TV and other members of the media following us. We were cat-called with ugly racial epithets all the way up the aisle. Outside we held a people's meeting on jobs.

When we returned in one hour, Minister Florence again asked whether Kodak would keep its promise, and the board chair just said, "No!" Minister Florence replied, "Then it will be a long, hot summer in Rochester." We marched out again, to the same chorus of racial curses. In the end, the bad publicity generated by the organized public pressure that FIGHT brought to bear forced powerful Kodak back to the table, and a new agreement was signed guaranteeing 600 new jobs for blacks in Rochester. There was one other casualty of this fight: John Mulder, the Kodak vice president who had signed the original agreement, was isolated and left the company after six months.

After the meeting, people were hugging the Lutheran pastor, patting him on the back, and thanking him for his church's hospitality to all 1,000 protestors that morning. He called several of us aside and said, "There is another special meeting tonight to see if I still have a job." He called us the next morning back in Rochester to say: "I won again, eight to seven!" One lone conservative Christian congregation followed the teachings of their leader, Jesus, that day, while the other denominations sinned. Organized people took on organized money—and won. Many years later, Minister Florence said, "Nothing has affected my life as profoundly as the FIGHT struggle." When a Detroit reporter asked Stokely Carmichael for an example of black power, he replied in three words: "FIGHT in Rochester."

Organizing in Chicago

At nineteen, I thought that rural Iowa and Minnesota were the real world. I knew there were big cities, but I hadn't experienced them. My first trip to Chicago opened my eyes and other senses to a new reality. I got on the Chicago "L" in the Loop with people looking like me, but I was headed for the black South Side. It was rush hour, and my car started out all white. I had my head in a book, and when I looked up near 22nd Street south the car was crowded, filling up with dark-skinned people. By 42nd Street, I was the only white in sight. I stood up instinctively, feeling that a black should get the seat, not me. It was like finding myself in a different world, as if I had suddenly found myself in Africa. As I got off the train looking for Friendship House on Indiana Avenue, I realized that I had been raised in relationships with selves like me and that I had better start learning about public ones. I had occasionally heard the "n word" but had never experienced a black community of thousands where I was the minority. I spent most of my formative days, from twenty to twenty-six in African-American communities. The local blacks treated me with respect and protected me.

You think college is where you got your education. Some of mine took place there, but nothing like what I got in the world as it is on the South Side of Chicago during the racial changes of the late 1950s and early '60s. Whole neighborhoods of Irish Catholic parishes were changing from all white to some blacks, and eventually all black, as white flight began. The Catholic bastion of "keep 'em out" was St. Leo's Parish at 78th and Emerald, a parish closed by the Archdiocese in 2002. The pastor there was Monsignor P. J. Molloy, the last of a dying breed. Cardinal Meyer made him join our ecumenical organizing drive to try and stabilize the area. Every Thursday, Monsignor Molloy had lunch with Mayor Daley at the Blackhawk Hotel downtown. About once a month, I'd get a phone call from him to drop whatever I was doing and get over to the rectory pronto.

On one occasion, I arrived about 10:30 in the morning. He'd already started drinking martinis and insisted that I have one. He was very talkative, showing off, and I was afraid that he was going to quit our organizing effort. I sipped one martini while he had a couple. Suddenly he jumped up and said, "Let me show you something." He had a private elevator in his newly built rectory, and down to the basement we went. After several minutes fumbling with a fist full of keys, he opened the sealed basement door. "Turn on the lights," he commanded. Groping in the dark, I found the bank of switches. The large basement room was absolutely empty except for something against the walls covered with white sheets. "Pick up the sheets," he ordered. Upon doing that, I found several beautiful religious paintings of nativity scenes and other things. "Monsignor," I exclaimed, "why aren't these hanging in the church?" P. J. replied, "I can't, friend of mine asked me to stash them here. It's hot art, but I have to get it out of here. Let's go have another drink." It's called social knowledge, which you only get from experiences like this.

At noon on another day, the phone rang. It was the monsignor. "Where's Chambers? I need him. We're going to the ball game." As I drove to Comiskey Park, Molloy's only instructions were, "Go faster." I started looking for a parking lot as we approach the park ten minutes before the game. We got near the main box office, with thousands of people rushing to enter, and Molloy said, "Drive right up there, over the curb." The Chicago cops saw Molloy's car and shoved the ordinary fans aside for him until we were twenty feet from the main entrance. "Leave the car, leave the keys, get lost," he said. "Be back here by the sixth inning, Mayor Daley and I will be finished with our business." Social knowledge education 101. When it came to the world as it is, the monsignor was a better teacher than Thomas Aquinas.

To Molloy's credit, he stood up for justice despite his personal bigotry. The founding meeting of the Organization of the Southwest Community (OSC) was scheduled to take place at Calumet High School with 2,000 South Siders, 99.6 percent white. Several days before the meeting, the credentials committee held an emergency meeting over the application of a small black Methodist congregation from the far northeast corner of the area. I had quietly talked the pastor of that church into applying for membership at the opening meeting. Then I asked Saul Alinsky to call the chancery office to urge

Cardinal Meyer to call Molloy and tell him to uphold Christian values, to wit, admit the black congregation; otherwise we would be building a segregationist organization on the South Side of Chicago.

At 7:00 P.M. on the Friday before the Sunday founding meeting, thirty-five key leaders crowded into our headquarters on West 79th Street. We had liberals, lots of moderates, and the conservatives (our language for the "keep 'em out" crowd), but nobody wanted to make the motion to exclude the black church. A Protestant minister was on an open phone line to his bishop for advice. Molloy and three other priests were there, all silent. The tension built. Dick Bukacheck, chairman of the credentials committee, entoned, "We also have a church application for admission from the northeast area. Is there a motion?" Dead silence. If there are a heaven and a hell, Judgment Day must feel like this. Finally, after what seemed like five minutes, Monsignor Molloy piped up, "I have some questions." You could have cut the air with a knife. "Is this a jack-leg preacher or a legitimate minister we're talking about?" Bukacheck answered, "He's an ordained minister." "Has he got a church in our area?" "Yes, monsignor, it's about a half-mile mile northeast of St. Leo's," Bukacheck responded. A long pause. "Then I move we let him in," said Molloy.

That Sunday afternoon, five minutes after the start of the founding meeting, a brave black pastor and six of his congregants walked down the aisle of Calumet High auditorium and took their seats up front. Molloy was the only one who could make that happen on the South Side of Chicago in 1958. Before he died, he mounted the pulpit one Sunday and apologized to the twelve or fifteen black families present in the pews for his bad racial language and attitudes. May he rest in peace with the other notorious Chicagoans. The Church is a religious institution with saints and sinners, but in the world as it is, it's often hard to tell which are which.

Making Organizing a Profession

Organizing in the 1950s and '60s was a low-paid, hair-shirt existence with long hours, heavy drinking, and a *machismo* style with its attendant bad habits. Then, as now, organizers learned by their own and other people's mistakes. In the early days, we had no training for leaders and a have-gun-will-travel approach for organizers.

There was no place for women in our organizing at first. I learned about rights and justice for women in the late 1950s and early '60s when organizing in the Woodlawn section of Chicago. I had been raised in a male clerical church and spent five years in a single-sex university and seminary. Scientists now tell us that we are all female in the womb for the first fifty-seven days of our time on this Earth, but I was raised believing that male was 100 percent male and female 100 percent female. There was no ambiguity on gender in the Iowa of my childhood or the single-sex higher educational institutions I had attended, but the needs and necessities of daily organizing in poor Chicago black neighborhoods and the strength of black females led me to hire three of them to make the organizing drives successful. They were better than the males I had inherited. Everything comes in pairs for a reason.

Alinsky had a misguided fix on marriage and females. He thought neither would work in the tough world of organizing. My continued experience contradicted this mindset, and when we started the IAF Training Institute, we cut women in on the same grounds and standards we had for men. Now no institution in twenty-first-century U.S. society bans women without being dragged into court for discrimination, except the Roman Catholic Church.

Alinsky's way of organizing started changing in the mid-1960s, when Dick Harmon, who had been organizing for Alinsky in Buffalo, and I pulled back from direct organizing to form a training center in Chicago. The decision to turn organizing in a professional direction began to take shape a few years before Alinsky died. At the conclusion of the Kodak fight in Rochester, Harmon and I realized that we would burn ourselves out if things kept on like this. We had to force Alinsky to institutionalize. He resisted at first; it wasn't his cup of tea. But we understood that if we did not take steps to institutionalize organizing as a profession, IAF's insights and work would die with Saul. I called him from Rochester and said, "Saul, I'm returning to Chicago to set up the IAF Training Institute. We need more organizers. I'm thirty-seven now and I'll burn out if we don't do this." There was silence. I explained a little more. Still silence. Then he asked, "Who is going to pay you?" "You are," I answered. "You will help raise the money, and I'll do the work." More silence. "I'll call in a couple of days," he said. His secretary called two days later with a message: "Saul said it's okay to move back to Chicago." At age thirty-seven, I had internalized a universal of successful politics: Go to power *with* a decision, never *for* a decision. Aimed action behind a decision gave birth to the modern IAF.

We got lucky when Gordon Sherman of Midas Mufflers contributed a quarter of a million dollars, and Saul had a contact with another foundation that got it matched. So Saul did his end of it, and in 1969 we opened up on North Michigan Avenue, where we began formation and training of professional organizers. I didn't know that Alinsky would be dead in three years. The reason I had pushed Saul into beginning to institutionalize was that I knew that if the universals of organizing that he had uncovered and wrote about were so critical to our society, we had to codify them in such a way that we could train men and women to organize. Harmon and I were burning ourselves out by organizing Saul's way. So we began the institutionalization, and when Saul dropped dead in 1972, the ball of wax was in our hands. By that time, the training institute was beginning to take off, and a lot of the good men that were with us then and the good women who began to join us are now running the key collectives that make up the IAF.

The early years of the institute were tough ones in America. Those were the days when movement hopes crashed as Americans started assassinating and killing icon leaders like John Kennedy, Malcolm X, Bobby Kennedy, and Martin Luther King. Watergate was not far away. So people began to ask, "What's the point of building movements and raising up heroes when they'll just kill them?" People in organizing had to get out or dig down inside themselves. At the institute, where we trained hundreds of people from around the country, participants began saying, "We've got to step up and mobilize and organize and take charge." We had to craft our social knowledge and experience of the universals of organizing very carefully into a mode and form that we could communicate to rookies. We also had to train in ways that would convince people with experience in the civil rights or antiwar movements that this training would allow them to take their energy and aim it into citizens organizations that would endure because they would be built around a dues base and the iron rule.

To teach and train ordinary people how to get a dynamic, effective public life, broad-based leaders have had the opportunity four times a year since the 1970s to attend ten days of national training with leaders from other cities and regions across the country. In these intensive sessions led by IAF's most experienced organizers, leaders tackle a practical and conceptual syllabus of social knowledge about public life, based on the collective wisdom gleaned from IAF organizing over the past sixty years. This training helps fill the vacuum of ignorance about public life in America. More than 400 people of all races, religions, and classes, and from countries throughout the world, avail themselves of this formation for public life and action each year. Ten-day training is a temporary retreat and withdrawal from everyday activity and commitments and an immersion in a university for public life. Some graduates return later to experience the formation again, but only after having returned home to act and reflect on what they have learned.

The training we developed is what allowed us to move from doing community organizing in the limited, turf-oriented sense to building broad-based citizens organizations. The training is for both professional organizers and key volunteer leaders, who learn the universals of organizing. They digest the experiences of public life that they are having back home and then turn it into social knowledge. At IAF national training, participants absorb in intensive, face-to-face sessions what you're reading in these pages.

IAF training helps people in both their private and public lives. A lot of leaders that we have attracted and kept with us take the know-how from IAF organizing and apply it on the job, often getting better jobs as a result. They know how to have a relational meeting with the boss. They know how to ask for a job two years in advance. They know how to get the slot that only white guys have ever held, by showing that they do most of the work anyway.

The major difference between early and modern IAF is that initially we did no training. We were very good during the civil rights movement at helping build black power organizations. After the actions, we would all go home, but we never stopped to evaluate. We never sat with leaders after actions to reflect on what we were doing, how we were doing it, what we could do better, what we could have changed, what we had learned. Building social knowledge through evaluation was not part of our ordinary way of doing business.

I had tried evaluating for years working with Saul, and now I had an opportunity to incorporate ten years of full-time organizing, not from theory to practice, but the other way around, from practice to theory. How could I take ten years of experience and digest it into workshops and seminars that would help young men and women develop their public skills? When we began the training institute, we didn't know how to teach the universals of organizing. Saul could talk about them, but he couldn't concretize them. Now we teach the universals of organizing, such as these guidelines:

- The iron rule: Never, never do for others what they can do for themselves.
- All action is in the inevitable reaction.
- All change comes about as a result of threat or pressure.
- Every positive has a negative, and every negative a positive.
- Action is to organization as oxygen is to the body.
- Never go to power for a decision, but only with a decision.
- The law of change: Change means movement; movement means friction; friction means heat; heat means controversy, conflict.
- Power precedes program.
- The opposition is your best ally in radicalizing your people.
- Anything that drags along for too long becomes a drag.
- Power without love is tyranny; love without power is sentimental mush.

- Your own dues money is almost sacred; other people's money starts controlling you.
- Power can never be conferred; it must be taken.
- The haves will never give you anything of value.
- Have-nots should not be romanticized; they cheat, lie, steal, double-cross, and play victim just like the haves do.
- Peace and justice are rarely realized in the world as it is; the pursuit, not possession, of happiness takes place amid struggle, conflict, and tension.
- Avoid cynics and ideologues; they have nothing to offer.
- Right things are done for wrong reasons, and bad things are often done for right reasons.
- Given the opportunity, people tend to do the right thing.
- Life force is about natality, plurality, and mortality.

Only leaders who gradually get the social knowledge embodied in these universals into their heart and guts can operate effectively in the public arena.

Creating the profession of organizing included a lot more than quality training. Decent salaries had to be paid. Health benefits and retirement plans had to be created. Proper vacations and sabbaticals had to be arranged. Most importantly, the needs and well-being of organizers' marriages and families had to be taken seriously. All these steps went in the opposite direction of the post–World War II culture of male *machismo*.

It has been a long, difficult struggle for the key organizers—Arnie Graf, Ernie Cortes, Mike Gecan, Christine Stephens, Gerald Taylor, Stephen Roberson, and the late Jim Drake—who made it happen over the last thirty years. What we learned to build is a new kind of collective in civil society—the broad-based citizens organization that I described in Chapter Three. I call the professionals whose task it is to build broad-based power democratic organizers.

Democratic Organizers

Democratic organizers are not fixers, deal-makers, spokespersons, or activists. They must have a high degree of social knowledge, native intelligence, anger, passion, and imagination. In the vernacular, they must have some fire in the belly and a willingness to go for the jugular.

I was in the Rio Grande Valley of Texas for a training session with leaders of Valley Interfaith. It was a Saturday morning with about 375 residents, many of them members of the local church where the meeting was being held. It was an important session, so much so that the bishop of the Rio Grande Diocese was present. The "antis" (right-wing reactionaries) were out to stop the organizing drive.

Twenty minutes after I started, the rear door swung open and an excited guy appeared. My two associates, Jim Drake and Ernie Cortes, said in chorus, "The antis are here." Without a thought, I took three steps down the center aisle with my finger aimed at our new visitor and shouted, "Who are you?" Surprised, he mumbled his name. Then I said, "You're not invited to this meeting." He retorted, "I'm a member of this parish." I responded, "This meeting is not for you. Please leave now." There was dead silence. He turned and walked out.

As the door closed, there was a spontaneous applause. When I concluded the session, a big, barrel-chested guy came up to me and said, "I want to shake your hand. I'm the football coach here and I was skeptical about this effort, but after the way you handled that trouble-maker, I'm with you all the way." The Bishop stroked me, too. "He's been nothing but trouble here for ten years." I felt pretty good.

An hour later I had to catch a flight to Chicago, so one of the women was designated to drive me to the airport because the training session was still going on. I thanked her for the ride and then dashed over to the check-in. As I bent over to put my piece of luggage on the belt for screening, I sensed I wasn't alone—three guys were following me now, and one of them was the "anti" I had thrown out. The cocky organizer was now scared. I thought, as they say in Texas, "I'm in deep shit here." They asked for my home address to mail me some literature. What if they get on the plane with me? What might they do to my wife and young daughters? I said, "I got to go. I got to go. My plane is leaving." On board, I told the stewardess I was a government agent being tailed by three men, and that I needed to stand near the door to make sure they didn't get on the airplane to Chicago. I never shared that one with my wife.

Organizing in the real world gets your hands dirty. Two memories come to mind. On the the racially tense Southwest Side of Chicago in the late 1960s, we held an election of the Organization of the Southwest Community (OSC). The chairman of the election committee was a young, right-wing real estate agent. My job was to watch him counting ballots. His candidate, a far out right-winger, missed being elected to the decision-making board of fifteen leaders by two votes. We looked at one another. I said, "I think we miscounted by three votes. This fifteenth liberal candidate was awarded those by mistake." We looked at each other again. "You're right," he said. My rationale was that we had too many liberals and not enough conservatives to keep the organization together.

In the 1980s, the first two Nehemiah homes in Brooklyn, New York, were constructed without a building permit. Getting those two houses built led to nearly 4,000 more built with proper permits. Sometimes you have to stretch morality with a venial sin. Our builder, I. D. Robbins, told organizer Mike Gecan that we didn't have a permit only after the construction had started. Mike and I discussed our bind: We were building two Nehemiah homes on city-owned land without a permit and our main sponsor was the renowned archbishop of Brooklyn, Francis Mugavero. Do we tell the archbishop or don't we? What a scandal for the church leader if we got caught. We shut up and prayed. This is how morality works in the messy real world. All action is ambiguous, never 100 percent good or bad.

In organizing, you will never die of boredom. It was a hot July evening in East Los Angeles in the mid-'80s. I was conducting a workshop for about 250 Hispanic leaders at St. Alphonsus Catholic Church. It was going smoothly until about 8:30, when there was a commotion in the rear. That seemed to settle down, when suddenly coming up the center aisle was a bulky Latino guy with a baton in his hand and a pair of white gloves on. I believe I was the only Anglo in the church basement. He marched toward me and then veered to my right and sat glaring at the group. Frantic Latino leaders from the rear were signaling time-out. I called for a break and went to the back, where Ernie Cortes informed me, "The gang is here, and they don't like a white talking to their people." With one eye on my gang visitor and attempting to stay cool, I continued the workshop for another fifteen to twenty minutes and then concluded the evening's events because of the heat. While people milled around, I slipped out the back door to a waiting car.

Organizing will lead you into strange, unpredictable situations. In 1986, I spent several weeks in apartheid South Africa, training black South Africans. My host, Ishmael Mkhabela, invited me to spend the weekend with his family in Soweto. We drove the fifteen miles from his office in Johannesburg to Soweto. He parked the car on a little pad in front of his very modest house. There were fifteen to twenty young people on the street in front of the house eyeing the tall white guy. The house was small and had no extra rooms, so I got the shed in back with a cot. After a nice meal, I retired to my cot in the shed. About 2 A.M. all hell broke loose—shouts, gunfire, return fire, more shouts. Panicked, I thought about leaving the shed and sprinting to the house. Instead, I crawled under the cot and straightened out the blanket so that it looked unoccupied. After about a half hour, things quieted down. I spent the rest of the night on the floor under the bed. The next morning at breakfast I learned what had happened. Neighbors had spotted two guys trying to steal Mkhabela's car and began shooting and shouting at them. Embarrassed, I never told my guest where I spent the night, nor my thoughts on who the shooters were looking for.

Organizers are agitators, catalysts, and public-life coaches. They stand for the whole. They make things happen. They are rooted in the holy books, democracy's founding documents, and the lives of public heroines and heroes. They are radicals in the best sense of the word. The "Why?" question is important to the professional organizer, who needs a nagging curiosity about how it is that people, events, and politics are this way or that way. They are generally feared and misunderstood for standing against the status quo. They are public people who seek collective power to act for justice. Being an organizer is not about being liked, but rather, as I have already said about public life, about being respected. Organizers march to a different drummer.

As I stressed in discussing relational meetings, the critical art of the organizer is selection. Organizing means an endless search for talent, passion, vision, and the ability to relate to other people. Organizers don't give people information or pander to their preferences. They push them to make a world they can believe in, not accepting things as they are, but pushing for things as they could be. Strong convictions attract some and repel others, but they don't leave people indifferent. Organizers agitate people to act on their values and interests in the world as it should be. Organizers teach engagement in public life as a means to moral meaning.

Organizers need to like tension, challenge, and people and to be able to dream new possibilities. It takes three to five years of full-time trial and error under a mentor before you "get it." Career organizing requires a network of organizers and leaders who hold you accountable. The organizer learns by mistakes—his or her own and other people's.

Activists and movement types are mobilizers and entertainers, not democratic organizers. Their script is their persona and their cause. They tend to be overinterested in themselves. Their understanding of politicalness is superficial or media-driven. They lack disinterestedness. They believe that the cause they lead is in the action—no dialectic, no subtleness, no ambiguity. Activists tend to be literal and narrow. They focus on problems, not issues, and their time frame is immediate. "What do we want?" "Freedom." "When do we want it?" "Now!" "No justice, no peace." Movement activists appeal to youth, frustrated idealists, and cynical ideologues, ignoring the 80 percent of moderates who comprise the world as it is. Moderates are not ideological.

They make decisions based on common sense and social knowledge. Sometimes they lean toward the left, sometimes toward the right.

Watch out for free-lance organizers. They gig you, they call the shot, they avoid reporting to you, they tend to have no discipline and generally no personal life. They cannot point to successes they've built. Go check them out where they say they have organized, talk to the local leaders about them, look for what they have built. Organizing is generational—not here today, gone tomorrow.

Values in Action

People know right from wrong, they just don't always act on it. We are usually trained by parents and religious institutions to suppress anger. Hot anger and rage are wrong. Apathy and resignation are wrong. There is an in-between—a cold anger—that is right on. In a document called "The Tent of the Presence," black pastors in the IAF spoke about such anger:

> Anger and grief are rooted in our most passionate memories and dreams—a father whose spirit has been broken by demeaning work or no work; a brother or sister lost to violence or alcohol or drugs; a church burned down by an arsonist; a college career sabotaged by a substandard high school; a neighborhood of shops and families and affections and relationships ripped apart because banks wouldn't lend to it, because insurance companies wouldn't insure it, because city officials wouldn't service it, because youth wouldn't respect us, because teachers wouldn't teach in it. Anger sits precariously between two dangerous extremes. One extreme is hatred, the breeding ground of violence. The other extreme is passivity and apathy, the breeding ground of despair and living death. Anger that is focused and deep and rooted in grief is a key element in the organizing of black churches.

Effective public-life organizers and leaders feel that anger, listen to it, and act on it.

In public life, tension is good. Bureaucrats spend their energy trying to eliminate tension. Big unilateral power avoids it. Its mindset is something like, "Try holding me accountable. I'm above that. That's why I have bodyguards, flak-catchers, and handlers. I only meet with powerful, sanitized, safe flatterers who tell me what I want to hear. How do you think I got where I am?"

Mature organizing requires a commitment to live in-between the two worlds. It's a vocation, a lifetime struggle with disappointments, failures, satisfactions, and moments of elation. Sophisticated organizing requires a historical understanding of the law of change and a creative imagination. There are ABCs of how to go about organizing. It's not the power you possess, but using the power of the opposition against itself that changes things. It's called political *jujitsu*. You must go outside the opponent's experience. You aim the action for the inevitable reaction, knowing that the reaction is more important than the action itself.

A typical day for professional organizers is not behind a desk or on the phone. They have to watch out for the phone and use it only to get dates for one-to-one, face-to-face relational meetings. When you walk unannounced into an office of bureaucrats, several of them will start picking up phones that aren't ringing to pretend they are busy. It's a universal—compounded by the cell-phone invasion: The products of the so-called electronic revolution are instruments created by the devil to keep us powerless.

The veteran organizer can sustain twenty-five to thirty relational meetings a week. Allies, potential enemies, and new contacts are all targets. The daily search of the organizer is for talent, energy, and vision. He or she understands that all organizing is constant disorganizing and reorganizing.

No one gets an organizer up in the morning, no one tells you whom to contact. No one holds you accountable every day. You are a self-starter. You use your imagination and creativity to get yourself in and out of trouble. You must be flexible and submerge your opinions. You are both a sponge and an agitator. Like the apostle Paul, you must have the ability and temperament to be to all things to all people. In the course of a week, you meet with a variety of personalities, attitudes, and prejudices—liberals, moderates, conservatives. When race is involved, you must be able to walk in other people's shoes. You must be respectful and knowledgeable about religious beliefs and customs. You must keep your private life separate from your public life. You must be genuinely interested in the other, not "tasky" or looking for your issues. You must be able to question, interrupt, and listen. Your senses are your tools— eyes, ears, nose, etc. Your most important gifts are intuition, instinct, and imagination. What you can't imagine concretely, you can't organize. You're a catalyst—looking, mixing, trying out different elements. Patience with others is critical, meeting them where they are, not where they should be, not where you are.

As an organizer, you fight becoming institutionalized. You refuse to sell. You present opportunities inside people's interests. You're always public, aware, and on guard. You're professional and don't share your private problems or anxieties. You are after a spirit connection with the other. You don't gravitate to the familiar, to those like yourself. You are not about making friends or finding soulmates. You're disciplined and focused on talent, ideas, the common good, and what the community could be.

What to Look For in an Organizer

So where do we find these professional organizers? The best organizers are mentored and in turn mentor others. Gender, faith, race, and marital or familial status are not issues, but age is. It's best to begin a career in organizing from ages twenty-four to twenty-six, but not before a person has some adult life experience to draw upon. There are all kinds of organizers—mothers of families, labor agents, ministers, teachers, CEOs, managers, politicians, etc.

Organizers have to be developed, but I look for certain traits. One is a high degree of native intelligence. Formal education and degrees are basically irrelevant. Avoid Ph.D.s. They can't act. They get lost in writing books for one another. They are good at a certain kind of analysis but never have a workable solution in the last chapter. For better or worse, at least a medical doctor gives you a prescription. Academic types are abstractionists. Does this make me anti-intellectual? No, I'm just warning you about theoreticians and overrated so-called experts.

The knowledge that matters for a potential organizer is social knowledge, which, as I've said repeatedly here, can only be gotten experientially, but it must be reflected upon. The stories in this book show that insight and wisdom arise from both success and failure—if they are evaluated. That grandparent of yours who never finished high school whom you check with on important decisions about marriage partners, medical operations, house purchases, and so on, has social knowledge.

Potential organizers should be successful at what they do, but restless and not satisfied. You spot them, whet their appetite, get them into the ten-day training experience, let them meet other leaders and organizers, and then proposition them to change careers. Try to pay a living wage.

Organizers need good intuition and imagination. That can't be taught. Some have it; some don't. This profession is for the few, not the many. Top-flight organizers are more like poets, symphony conductors, or other creative artists than typical professionals or managers.

Organizers need some anger. *Angr* is an Old Norse word meaning "grief" or "memory." Anger is your engine, and it resides below the belly button. It gets you going, compels you to challenge things as they are. "That's not right." "Don't use that word when you talk about blacks." "What's going on here, officer?" "Who told you that lie?"

Organizing for Family, Society, and Plurality

The social world and the people who inhabit it are not one and the same. Society lies between people and supports them and their civic organizations. Our present world is dominated by a scientific, technological, consumerist world view driven by global capitalism. The line in the fight about how the world should be is now drawn between market values and generational ones. In this war of values, professional organizers are committed to action in the public realm and to political judgment. Their theory must be relentlessly and ruthlessly concrete because concreteness is a foundational ground for wise political judgment.

Democracy cannot work without the units essential to its operation— families, congregations, labor unions, and organized collectives of citizens who act in public life for justice and the common good. The organizer's task is to connect those smaller units of civil-society power into collectives that have the ability to hold elected officials and corporations accountable. The challenge organizers face is that the average American is an individualist who doesn't see public life as a vocation. But religious and democratic values are grounded in the idea and reality of communities of people for whom public life must be part of mission and citizenship. Public life has to be something that people work at and have vocational meetings about, something centered around the issues and values that they feel are important. Organizing means seeing to it that what should happen in accordance our values does happen. That's how this country was built, and it's the vocation of professional organizers to see that the building continues and improves.

7

Broad-Based Organizing for the Twenty-First Century: United Power for Action and Justice

> "There is price to be paid for any genuine pluralism. . . . It is that there is no longer a center. There are many. . . . The others must become genuine others to us—not projections of our fears and desires."
>
> DAVID TRACY

Disposable Cities

Like all of America's cities, Chicago grew haphazardly in the previous century. The city was laid out commercially in a grid pattern. That later allowed automobiles to skip through and around self-contained neighborhoods. Chicagoland became one of America's great industrial areas, building its economy on manufacturing jobs. Today, obsolete commercial structures and abandoned buildings line mile after mile of central-city streets. The suction of suburbs and their malls, coupled with planned shrinkage and redlining of older sections of the city, gutted the life out of old neighborhoods. From 1967 to 1987, Chicago lost 60 percent of its manufacturing jobs. That means that more than 320,000 households lost their primary source of employment. The same thing happened in Philadelphia, New York, Detroit, and other urban areas.

In the early 1960s, the first Mayor Daley pledged to eliminate slums in ten years. What happened instead was that slums grew, especially after the riots following Martin Luther King's killing. The vacant land and abandoned buildings on the Westside and South Side of Chicago grew. The emphasis in the '90s was on expensive high-rise condos, while affordable homes and rental housing disappeared. It's a developers' profit-making paradise, with the poor, immigrants, and low-wage workers squeezed out by gentrification. The Near-North Side of the city became a jungle of derricks and closed walking space. All the creative energy of city officials and state government has gone into getting a third runway at O'Hare Airport and expanding the McCormick Convention Center.

Our disposable society is quick to throw out the places and traditions from which it arose. Today's speed and mobility serve the wealthy on the fast track, but most people live in modest homes and struggle to keep their households together and supplied with the basic necessities of life. As a nation, we are more creative with military weapons and financial instruments than with our decaying urban base. This shouldn't be a surprise because pollsters tell us that the balance of political power has moved to the suburbs. So there are senators and members of Congress for corporations, farmers, oil and gas, military, business and finance, and developers, but none for America's great cities. Can these large, sprawling urban centers of two to five million residents with their two- to three-hour daily commutes and failing public schools have a human future?

In the twenty-first century, a critical challenge to cities will be to help those who are already here welcome the new immigrants and to figure out how to fold them into the social fabric of our cities. A city like Chicago, with new Hispanic, Asian, and Muslim immigrant populations flooding in, is not going to thrive if we don't figure out how to integrate the newcomers. They're the fastest-growing population segments. Both black and white population numbers are on the decline. That's not just Chicago's story—it's America's. The plurality I discussed in a previous chapter is here, and more is on the way. The organizers and leaders of broad-based organizations must not only embrace differences but also teach others how to do the same.

During the 1980s and '90s, the IAF network through its affiliates built sections of new cities in a number of America's most devastated urban areas. The social knowledge gained in doing that led me to try something different in Chicago. Rather than working in a section of the city, or even the whole city of Chicago, we set out to build the largest metropolitan citizens organization ever attempted to that point by bringing city and suburbs together under one big tent. On October 19, 1997, at the founding assembly of a new broad-based citizens organization called United Power for Action and Justice, the following statement of purpose was adopted by 10,000 leaders from religious, labor, and civic institutions from across Chicagoland.

> Our purpose is to create a broad-based organization whose goal is to build relational power for collective actions in the name of justice and the common good. We are an organization of other organizations, weaving together the city and its suburbs. We are inclusive, embracing the full diversity of metropolitan Chicago. As part of civil society, we are nonpar-

tisan: moderates, conservatives, liberals, and radicals committed to acting
on our social values and working for a just society by standing for the
whole. We are generational: originating, not just reacting, and sustaining
as a legacy for the future our dedication to fostering public life.

That assembly included blacks, whites, Latinos, and Asians; Christians, Jews,
Muslims; city residents and suburbanites; members of faith-based institutions, secular folk, and labor union members. Chicago media called it the
most diverse collective of citizens ever assembled in Chicago. A newness was
born that day. As citizens came together to exercise the natality that I described earlier, the air was full of creative excitement and hope. A half hour
before the assembly was called to order, one of United Power's primary leaders said, "This is like my wedding day." But the story of IAF in Chicago
begins nearly forty years before the founding assembly of United Power.

Deep Roots in the Windy City

Chicago was the birthplace of Saul Alinsky's IAF, beginning with the Back of
the Yards Neighborhood Council in 1939. It was our home base until 1978,
when I relocated the national headquarters to New York to shore up efforts
in New York and Baltimore. Chicago citizens only had Back of the Yards and
The Woodlawn Organization (TWO) as viable citizen groups, but they were
no longer affiliated with IAF.

Beginning in 1991, Monsignor Jack Egan, an IAF trustee, was pressuring
me to return to Chicago and build a modern IAF citizens operation. Part of
me felt guilty, having spent nearly thirteen years of my life organizing in
Chicago. IAF needed a Midwest base. Jack called me with what he thought
was great news: "Ed, I've got a two-million-dollar commitment from a major
foundation if you'll bring IAF back to Chicago." "Jack," I pleaded, "that's no
good. It's the wrong sponsorship. We need denominational funds to launch
something that is broad-based and inclusive. A millionaire's foundation is no
good." I deflated but didn't stop him. "So tell me, how would you go about
it?" he asked me. Challenged, I had to come up with something. "Get me the
names of young Jack Egans," I said, "and include priests from the suburbs,
not just inner-city priests. I'll come back for two days in a couple of months
and meet with them and also with some African-American pastors separately.
Unless Roman Catholics and black Baptists and Pentecostals are interested,
and have their judicatories put up sponsoring money, it won't work."

It was spring of 1993. Goethe's warning that "the only free step is the first
one" had somehow slipped my mind. After that first, free step you get

trapped. For a year and a half, I flew in every two months for a couple of days, returning to the most segregated big city in the U.S., which I didn't relish. Too much pain, too many memories, too many hopes and fears. My consolation was that I had someone in mind who could do the actual organizing without any financial worries after I'd raised the money for three years of operations. Flying in and out—trying to figure out where there was money without strings and who would put it up for a pig in a poke. Sponsoring committees for new organizations are not built around crass self-interest but at best operate around enlightened self-interest or even doing the right thing for the wrong reason. I proposed to raise $2 million-plus for the Chicago Metropolitan Sponsors; then, of course, I had to raise it.

The outsider flying in and out with a new approach is a tacit insult to local organizations and leaders who live and plan to raise families there. Being the "Second City" and in the Midwest, Chicago suffers from an inferiority complex. The city establishment welcomed Boeing's move to Chicago with the governor and mayor standing obsequiously at the foot of the ramp when the executives landed, but an outside radical from the Alinsky tradition is looked upon with suspicion and skepticism. I was greeted with a litany of reactive stereotypes: "You can't raise that kind of money for Chicago organizing." "You don't understand about Chicago neighborhoods." "Suburban folks won't work with city people." "Cook County and the city together in one organization won't work—it's too big." "Chicagoans' comfort zone is their turf, the mall, the Bulls, the Magnificent Mile." "You'll learn that North Siders never go to the South Side." "We moved to the suburbs to get away from the city." "The West Side is the best side—don't tell me about black preachers on the South Side."

The only people thinking and acting metropolitan-wide in the Chicago area were business and corporate types. Early on, while I was flying in and out on two-day trips, I met with three officers of the Civic Committee of the Commercial Club of Greater Chicago. The meeting was friendly, and they showed some interest in the scope and the scale of what I was raising local money for. They knew about Alinsky's IAF and had heard about our New York and Texas efforts. It was a courtesy call, describing a kind of citizens organization they were unfamiliar with. Toward the end of the meeting, one of them said, "We know about IAF's ability to organize 8,000 to 10,000 people in one place at one time on one issue. If you can figure out how to get us a third runway at O'Hare, maybe we can work together." I stressed that we were not at that point yet. These creative, entrepreneurial businessmen had a vision that included the city and suburbs, six counties. They instinctively understood broad-based organizing.

The linchpin of success in this effort was the black Pentecostal and Baptist preachers and my old ties to The Woodlawn Organization and its former president, Reverend Arthur M. Brazier, now Bishop Brazier with a congregation of over 13,000 members. Would the blacks trust the whites one more time? These were the days after Mayor Harold Washington, who had climbed the mountain of Chicago politics and brought the black community with him. But a white Irish politician, the son of Mayor Richard J. Daley, had removed the mountain, when he became Washington's successor.

I knew the African-American pastors had total veto power over any new effort, no matter how much Cardinal Bernardin committed. We held four or five sessions during 1993 and 1994 on the South Side. The key players were Bishop Brazier, Reverend Clay Evans, Reverend Addie Wyatt, and Reverend Leon Finney, Jr. They weren't interested unless the cardinal put up $1 million and they would match that with $300,000 of their own money. Getting $1 million out of a diocese that was closing churches and schools for lack of funds would not be easy.

With some movement from the African-American Baptists and Pentecostals, I intensified my efforts with the Catholics and the mainline Protestants. I did sessions with Jack Egan's suggested city and suburban pastors, but I had to run an action on Egan. I told him his place was the sidelines—no more of the brokering he'd been doing for forty years. It hurt him, but he listened and let others pin the cardinal when the time came. Eight key pastors were trained to confront and nail down $1 million from Cardinal Bernardin. At the meeting with him, after describing the plight of their neighborhoods and their ministries and the failure of the Catholic laypeople in the suburbs to do justice, the pastors laid their request on the table. The cardinal pleaded no money. He pleaded having to close some schools. They countered, "Get the money from your connections. Go outside your finance committees. Go to the National Catholic Campaign for Human Development. Go to Chicago-based religious orders of men and women. Go to the cemetery fund and endowments." He got the picture and went to work. In four months' time, the pastors had the cardinal's commitment, to be paid over three years.

The mainline Protestants were no easier. We struck out with the Presbyterians and the Methodists. We had a breakthrough with the conservative Lutheran Church Missouri Synod—$600,000. That in turn helped with the Evangelical Lutheran Church of America for a similar amount. The Jewish community pledged a smaller amount. Some movement was happening. After these commitments, we invited the Muslims and labor unions on board. They also delivered their funds.

Whenever the interreligious principals got together, they were always polite and sympathetic to one another; the prophets and visionaries were never in the room. At the critical commitment meeting, I needed reinforcements to push Cardinal Bernardin to lead with his $1 million. No lead from the Catholic Church, no deal. I imported a burly Italian-American priest, Father Dom Grassi, who had been part of the original meeting of the cardinal with his priests. At our committee meeting of about a dozen principals from seven denominations, this Catholic pastor was instructed to sit directly across from the cardinal and stare at him for one hour and fifteen minutes, saying nothing. After some hemming and hawing, the cardinal popped for the million. The white Protestants followed, and the African-American ministers nailed down the deal. A Chicago metropolitan sponsoring committee came into existence with three years of funding, credentialed by an important cross-section of Chicagoland's religious leaders. Over coffee after the meeting, I conferred an IAF "Oscar" on Father Grassi.

Once the religious leaders were on board, it was important that the mayor of Chicago hear about the new organization, including its strategy for affordable homes for working Chicago families. The Reverend Finney, Bishop Brazier, and Cardinal Francis George (successor to Cardinal Bernardin) met with Mayor Daley at city hall. The mayor knows all about local neighborhood organizations and how to deal with them. He only snapped to attention when the word "suburbs" was mentioned. Once it was made plain that we were pursuing a city-and-suburbs strategy from the get-go, his interest was piqued. At the end of the meeting, the mayor said that he understood our strategy and thought it would help the metropolitan area—if it worked. He was astute enough to understand that there are some things even the mighty city of Chicago can't do alone.

After this groundwork was laid, my problem became, who's going to organize this? Because of family concerns, my original candidate, an IAF supervisor in another city, was unavailable. So in my sixty-fifth year, with lots of pressure on my family life, I selected myself. My family had moved to Ireland several years earlier and expected me to retire there soon. A public/private dilemma. Was it a mistake for me? Probably. Unfair for my wife and five young children? Probably. They came back and lived with me for three years during the building of United Power for Action and Justice and then returned to Ireland. Job, of the Hebrew scriptures, is my only consolation: "All life is an eternal struggle."

How did we staff the organizing project? I got lucky and transferred an experienced veteran from New York to Chicago as lead organizer, Stephen Roberson. I hired a rookie from Boston, Cheri Andes, who performed outstandingly. And I hired the best of the local Chicago organizers, Josh Hoyt, an ingenious person. The four of us did relational meetings week after week for two years and got 250 leaders trained and doing the same. Two years and 13,000 relational meetings later, United Power for Action and Justice was born in November 1997 in an assembly of more than 10,000 citizens at the University of Illinois/Chicago Pavilion. Our only snag was when a six-foot guy appeared lugging a ten-foot cross and claiming to be Jesus. Arnie Graf, one of our veteran organizers, who happens to be Jewish, stopped the so-called Jesus as he approached an entrance, demanding to know what he was all about. The guy replied, "I'm Jesus, and I'm going inside." "You can't," Graf replied. "Jesus is already inside." A nod to the cops and the guy with the ten-foot cross disappeared. Citizens in action protected their democratic assembly.

In the creation of United Power, intentionality, initiation, patience, and a broad inclusive vision prevailed over movement, reaction, the quick fix, and media events. Connecting people around values, talent, and energy won out. In the most segregated urban center in America, a racial mix, an interfaith mix, a city and suburban mix, a labor union and business mix were crafting a metropolitan agenda benefiting the poor, working poor, middle class, and wealthy, a broad-based organization of other organizations combining talents and efforts for the common good. The central strength of United Power is its mix of some committed liberals and conservatives with about 75 percent moderates, folks who on any given issue lean more or less right or left. As ideologues of left and right disappear, the future in America is for stand-up and standout moderates, and United Power leaders understand that.

United Power in Action

Like its sister organizations in metropolitan Boston, Dallas, and Los Angeles, United Power is applying the universals developed by the IAF over the past sixty years to organizing citizen power on a scale that has not been attempted before. As the twenty-first century begins, United Power has more than 330 active, dues-paying member organizations. Because United Power is an organization of organizations, these 330 institutions represent thousands of individual leaders throughout metropolitan Chicago. United Power's member organizations now include congregations, labor unions, and civic organizations. Leaders meet and act locally, in geographic clusters called assemblies. Each local assembly chooses representatives who together constitute United Power's Steering and Strategy Team, which sets policy and determines the organization's agenda. This body elects an Administrative Team to handle organizational matters, hold organizers accountable, and research topics prior to their consideration by the Steering and Strategy Team.

Local training and formation sessions are held monthly throughout the city and suburbs on how to research, craft problems into specific, concrete actions, and hold relational meetings, followed by group reports. Advanced leaders learn to conduct house meetings, where eight to ten people unknown to one another meet for sixty to ninety minutes in someone's home or a church basement to share and discuss social issues. Assemblies and forums are then created to deal with those issues. Citizen leaders take turnout quotas for those public meetings for their organizations. Taking these steps initiates the public work of an organization. IAF sponsors strategic planning sessions six to eight times a year for experienced leaders of United Power. Retreats where leaders draw off for a day and a half of evaluation and reflection are conducted seasonally. Teaching citizens to get out the vote and do sign-up and take-charge campaigns is another way that United Power fosters the development of its members' politicalness. Assisting member organizations in their struggles is also important work done by staff and key leaders.

What has this organization of organizations accomplished?

United Power's Gilead Campaign for the Uninsured addresses the fact that one in every seven Illinois residents has no health insurance. Phase I of the campaign established the Gilead Outreach and Referral Center to help medically uninsured individuals get coverage under existing programs. Phase II is focused on expanding affordable primary care. Phase III will be an effort to expand insurance options, including family care, and to enhance private-sector choices. Within its first four years, United Power linked 15,000 individuals to health care and won the governor of Illinois's support for Family Care, a comprehensive health-care plan for all citizens of Illinois. It convened a meeting of state and federal officials with more that 1,400 United Power leaders at the State of Illinois building, followed by a three-month communications and canvassing campaign to dramatize citizen support for Family Care. United Power won overwhelming support for Family Care legislation in the state legislature, including a unanimous vote in the House and a majority of senators as legislative cosponsors. It secured an executive order from Governor Ryan seeking a federal waiver to obtain funding earmarked for Family Care coverage for 80,000 working parents.

Ezra Community Homes is United Power's initiative to increase housing options for working families. Ezra doesn't just plug individuals into available slots; it transforms large tracts of vacant land into vibrant neighborhoods, while helping residents become confident homeowners. Ezra helps homeowners join with their neighbors in establishing productive relationships with elected officials, police and fire departments, local businesses, and others. Drawing on the social knowledge developed by the IAF over the past twenty-five years, beginning with the Nehemiah homes in New York, United Power's goal is to build thousands of affordable homes for low- and moderate-income working families over a ten-year period. The organization secured $5.2 million in interest-free loans to fund home construction, won passage of a Chicago city council ordinance to authorize property transfers for 140 sites in a devastated Westside area of the city, conducted homeowner education sessions with more than 300 interested individuals, prescreened the first prospective Ezra buyer families, qualified the first group for Ezra financing and subsidies, and secured a signed contract from the city's Commission on Housing, which authorized groundbreaking on 140 sites in North Lawndale for construction of the first Ezra homes for working families.

Through United Power organizing, including a working relationship with a member of Congress, significant assistance has also been secured from the federal government to assist metropolitan Chicago's homeless. These funds will go toward support services, including mental health and addiction recovery counseling. The program will provide services and measure their effectiveness in breaking the cycle of homelessness. The U.S. Department of Health and Human Services authorized $921,000 for a national demonstration grant to assist Chicago's homeless. Like the $1 million grant that United Power won to assist the homeless in Lake and Northwest suburban Cook Counties, these funds will go toward support services, including mental health and addiction recovery counseling. The program will both provide services and measure their effectiveness in helping to break the cycle of homelessness.

Following the launch of United Power in Chicago, the IAF and two veteran United Power leaders—Tom Lenz in Lake County and Katie Poronsky in DuPage County—have been developing two new and different sponsoring committees. As a result of informing themselves and experiencing United Power at work, citizen leaders from these two counties want their own countywide organizations. Lake and DuPage Counties should have founding conventions by mid-2003. Statewide issues cannot be won without organizing several more metropolitan Chicago counties, as well as some downstate.

The greatest successes of this kind of organizing never get into print or on TV because, like democracy, they only exist in moments. The fact is that Chicagoans have a new twenty-first century institution that is unique and different in its scope, scale, and inclusiveness; one that eliminates the fear of the stranger, of people who don't look like us; that works in practical ways day in and day out to close racial divides; that builds tolerance for other beliefs and traditions; that allows people to share stories with one another;

that respects the nonchurched; and that gives people a chance to pray together. These are the facts that don't make media reports. United Power leaders know that unless people *act* together there is no bond, no solidarity, no justice. Right now in Chicagoland, low-wage earners and upper-class suburbanites who are mixed together by United Power are in a conversation about their struggle. These kinds of moments are happening and will continue to happen. Connecting, relating, experiencing one another, being vulnerable, and getting turned on to public life is the social dynamic that United Power creates.

Chicago's Answer to 9/11

Like most Americans, I was paralyzed for two days after the World Trade Center attack. A cold anger came over me when TV talking heads began hyping Pearl Harbor as the metaphor for 9/11. "No, no," I shouted at the TV. The metaphors on crossing this line are Hiroshima and Nagasaki, where the U.S. government put atomic bombs on our airplanes and dropped them on Japanese citizens, killing and radiating hundreds of thousands. We are the only country to incinerate thousands with nuclear violence, not to mention Dresden, Cambodia, and Vietnam. Fifty years before 9/11, the U.S. has been there, done that. Our arrogance about our real-world behavior is unbelievable.

But what could United Power do about 9/11? Could we create an alternative to the flag waving and "hug a Muslim" stuff being played out elsewhere? Fortunately, we had a starting place called relationships. Chicago has never been kind to immigrants—the Polish, Irish, Jews, Lithuanians, Hispanics, and especially the blacks from the Southern states, who flocked there during and after World War II. These groups have had to continue fighting their way into equality, freedom, and opportunity. I deliberately initiated United Power's relationships with the new immigrant Muslim community of metropolitan Chicago from the organization's beginning. There are more than 400,000 new immigrants of the Islamic faith living in metropolitan Chicago. Talat Othman, a Muslim business leader, tells this story about how these new immigrants got engaged with United Power.

> Over the past fifteen years, our numbers have been swollen by immigrants from thirty-five countries around the world. During 1995, a Christian man called several of our leaders to request a meeting with us. We hesitated, but he insisted and wanted to meet us at our places of worship. We finally agreed, and these meetings took place at seven

or eight different mosques around metropolitan Chicago over the next year.

This outsider talked to us about building a new and different kind of citizens organization and said that this was the ground floor. Christian and Jewish religious groups were organizing a city/suburban citizens' effort, and he wanted us on board at the beginning with members and money. He said that they needed us as much as we needed them, needed our power, our money, and our culture mixed with theirs. He spoke to us in an up-front, straightforward way. We had been looking for a way to get involved in the broader Chicago community, but felt cautious and hesitant.

So when someone asks me why 200 Muslim leaders joined with more than 9,000 Jewish, Christian, and secular leaders in October 1997 for the public founding of United Power for Action and Justice, and why 2,000 of our people came together with 2,000 Christians in a public assembly two months after 9/11, my answer is that it's because this man, Ed Chambers, recognized and respected us by first coming to us from the larger, unknown community, and then inviting our participation. It's that simple.

Building on that history, I called a small caucus meeting with Talit Othman and the other Muslim leaders who had joined in the founding of United Power. We met in a mosque in the Loop. I chaired the meeting and laid down some ground rules. No discussion of international issues like Israel and Palestine or Iraq. We would focus on Chicagoland: What could we do to respond to 9/11 as citizens here in our homeland? As the ninety-minute meeting proceeded, we talked about an event at which Muslims and non-Muslims would address the Koran's teachings on suicide, violence, and tolerance. The seven key Muslim leaders were tentative and insecure about the response of the majority group of Chicagoans. Two days later at a strategic planning session of United Power's non-Muslim leaders, I shared the thoughts of the Muslim caucus. The Chicago majority group also wanted to do something but felt mixed and confused. A possible event to be held in two months was discussed centering around "Chicagoans and Islam." A turnout target of 4,000 was discussed, a fifty-fifty mix of Muslim and non-Muslim.

Preplanning went on for the next six weeks. Quotas were taken, and training sessions were conducted at the Muslim mosque on how to do turnout. A public drama was invented as the program for the event, and a floor team was chosen and trained. After much debate a neutral, prominent site, the Festival Hall on Navy Pier, was chosen. A Sunday afternoon from 1:30 to 3:00

was selected. Three weeks before the scheduled assembly, the team came up with a stroke of genius: "Let's bring our teenagers. This problem is long-range and generational; we adults are not going to solve it by bombing Afghanistan or Iraq."

On November 18, with no public promotion, 4,000 Chicagoans met, including 750 teenagers. Our big fear was a bomb threat, which would have wiped out all our careful planning and produced the opposite outcome of what we intended. Ushers scattered arriving delegations so that seats were left open beside people for someone they didn't know. Breaking up congregations from the suburbs wasn't easy. Busloads of Muslim groups from the Southwest Side wanted to sit together; trained Muslim ushers broke them up.

The meeting was co-chaired by Muslim and majority-group leaders. The event began and ended with Muslim and non-Muslim leader pairs speaking to each other on stage about their cultures, families, and why they came to this event. Its centerpiece was 2,000 one-to-one relational meetings between 4,000 Muslim and non-Muslim participants lasting twenty-five minutes each. Self and other, Muslim and non-Muslim, city and suburb dialogued. The action began with one black leader reading an excerpt from the Declaration of Independence and ended with 4,000 people reading the same passage in unison. It was social dynamite.

The public action was rated as "A–." It was talked about for months. People who didn't come were confronted on what they had missed. Follow-up sessions were scheduled in five different regions of metropolitan Chicago. This was a citizens' coming-out event for plurality and otherness, during which thousands of Chicagoans put a face on the other. It depolarized the Muslim/non-Muslim tension being felt everywhere in Chicago, and those who participated started to feel differently because of a face-to-face meeting with a formerly unknown and different fellow citizen of the Windy City. Media coverage was intense. Four thousand organized Chicagoans acted while the government bombed Afghanistan and the stock market took a dive. United Power gave witness that day to a twenty-first-century Chicago that ought to be a lesson for the whole nation. November 18 was Chicago's answer to 9/11.

8

Thoughts on Twenty-First-Century Challenges

"The dogmas of the quiet past are inadequate to the stormy present. As our case is new, so we must think anew and act anew."
ABRAHAM LINCOLN

The American Crisis

The so-called free market is probably on a course of self-destruction. There have to be boundaries on Wall Street, or all the money flowing to the top 10 percent and taken away from the bottom 60 percent, will lead to a fractured civil society. Twenty-first-century Americans must rid ourselves of the legal fiction of the corporation as person and the marketeers' clever illusion that the market is the "private sector." This is nonsense. Outfits like Enron, Arthur Andersen, and WorldCom are public; they make the public suffer by being crooks and cheats. And they are just the tip of the iceberg. One thousand companies have filed with the Securities and Exchange Commission to revise their auditing reports since 1995. By the time this book comes out, things are going to be worse.

It's the job of the state to put boundaries on the market—in other words, to hold it accountable for the common good. Without an organized civil society, the state becomes a servant of the market. The Enron/Arthur Andersen/Bush version of crony capitalism is a major scandal, but only the beginning. As Simon Caulkins stated in a *London Observer* op-ed piece on February 3, 2002:

> As management crashes go, Enron rates a faultless 10. It has everything, but in reverse. Instead of creating value, jobs, pensions, and lives, it has destroyed them. As well as ruining the reputation of business-school professors, it could well pull down its auditor, the giant Arthur Andersen. Governments could even be dragged under too.
>
> Enron provides a fitting epitaph to the bubble decade of the 1990s. It is also a quintessential fable for our time, pointing up with black-and-

white clarity the Faustian battle now being waged for the corporate heart and soul. As Enron shows, it's a battle that the devil can still win—and even now is busy turning into a damage-limitation exercise, with sooth-ing suggestions about tighter auditing and better nonexecutive directors.

This is like saying you can stop people joining al-Qaeda with better passport controls. The truth is that Enron was way past technical control, being the living embodiment of the fundamentalist management beliefs that took hold in the 1990s, with results that are now nightmarishly plain.

We must see capitalism for what it is—who benefits, who suffers, and its limitations.

Left to itself, capitalism will self-destruct while the politicians of the state are busy genuflecting to it. Lester Thurow, a professor at the Massachusetts Institute of Technology's Sloan School of Management, has warned us about the inevitable unfairness of capitalism: "The first and best solutions are to warn all small investors that the game is rigged. No individual investor, no matter how well informed, can play on the same level as the major institu-tional investors, Wall Street firms, and corporate executives, who receive more accurate information more quickly than the average viewer of CNBC." Greed and getting rich on the backs of others have been the constant companions of modern capitalism. The 1990s bubble didn't change a thing. Presidents Reagan and the two Bushes trash government and cut regulatory budgets.

In the early 1980s Sheldon Wolin, America's finest political teacher, fore-warned us about the inequity of our democracy's leading institutions.

> Every one of the country's primary institutions—the business corpora-tion, the government bureaucracy, the trade union, the research and edu-cation industries, the mass propaganda and entertainment media, and the health and welfare system—is anti-democratic in spirit, design, and operation. Each is hierarchical in structure, authority oriented, opposed in principle to equal participation, unaccountable to the citizenry, elitist and managerial, and disposed to concentrate increasing power in the hands of the few and to reduce political life to administration.

Today we would add Wall Street, the so-called free market, and the U.S. economy.

Right now, the middle class is falling back into the working class, and the working class is falling back into serious debt. As the growth of the poor and dispossessed in America continues, its majority population struggles from day to day despite working two or three jobs per household. Jobs are being taken away from men and women who have worked twenty to twenty-five years for a corporation. Of course, the euphemism is "downsized." The French word for downsizing means "de-greasing." It's closer to the truth. You're out, and you'll never get that job back. And this is now happening even to lawyers and accountants, the secure professions, the career ladders that our fathers and mothers were promised after World War II. Now there's no ladder for the downsized to climb. This is creating tremendous pressure on families and children.

In one of our Chicago-area assemblies, a woman told a story of being forced back to work because her husband had been downsized, their savings running out, and her husband finding another job at $40,000 or $50,000 less than what he had been making. Her story ends with their not being able to send their two daughters back to college. Throughout America, there are clusters of men meeting in support groups on Wednesday nights to tell one another that it's not their fault. These men turn to alcohol, drugs, depression, and abuse because they have given up on themselves. They were told that they were somebody, now they're booted out and they think that they're nobodies. That's why the have-nots want to become have-a-littles. Society has built an underclass, and there are a lot of people among the have-nots. Building prisons is a solution to absolutely nothing. There are over a million African-American men in prison today; are we going to go to two million? We're privatizing and we're downsizing, and we'll pay for it, now or later.

If society doesn't put safety nets under core institutions, you're not going to have a next generation coming up with much to look forward to. Eventually, the money flow going to a select elite will crash. But the big abuse is that the wealthy are buying the government. The amount of money that's being used by American-controlled and foreign multinationals to purchase influence with both political parties, and the involvement of lobbyists in drafting legislation by congressional committees, is obscene. As President Eisenhower recognized in his warning about the military-industrial complex, big money has always influenced government, but not in the form of the immediate access that money buys today. The free-marketers are reigning and ruling the minds and hearts of Congress members and presidents.

Someday, Americans will see that civil society, not economic man, is the necessary centerpiece of a real democracy. The economy either aids and abets civil society by supporting its mediating institutions like families, unions, congregations, hospitals, and school systems, or it doesn't. Economic self-interest won't work as society's glue. Contracts can't hold a society together. There's globalization going on. The commodification of our public life is rampant. Corporate America knows no boundaries; its capital is mobile. But residents of New York or Texas or California or Chicago are not that mobile.

They are rooted; they live in places and have traditions. We are generational people; we don't exist in nanoseconds, like the foreign exchange market that can move $1.7 trillion in a day.

We have to rebuild and reorganize the mediating structures that are under attack, just as we always have to do. The family is under attack. Behind the smoke screen of "family values" rhetoric, there is little or no respect for the bonding institutions of kinship and family, procreation and nurturing. The social capital generated by marriage, parenting, and caring for elderly relatives is rarely celebrated. There is not an American commitment to the family as we find in Europe.

The so-called welfare reform of the 1990s is obscene, especially in light of the growing information we have on things like critical brain development that principally takes place in the first three years of an infant's life. It's getting clearer every day that critical development won't take place in young people at age seven or age thirteen, if it isn't grounded in what happens in the first three years. Given information like that, I don't know why we're not paying mothers to stay home and nurture their kids, hold and talk to them, rather than forcing mothers out of the home and into low-wage jobs. But no, we're getting mothers off welfare, displacing working poor. So the working poor go somewhere else, maybe to welfare, and the welfare mothers go back to welfare. "Work first" puts families and children last.

You can't undo the New Deal, especially Social Security. We have learned something, and people's social knowledge says that the New Deal was good for the U.S. The *Chicago Tribune* under Colonel McCormick opposed Roosevelt's policies. On the day that the state of Delaware adopted Social Security, one year before the federal government did, McCormick went to the flagpole at the top of the Tribune Towers, took down the American flag flying there, and cut Delaware's star out of the flag. After desecrating the flag, he ran it back up to the top of Tribune Towers with only forty-seven stars. Now Social Security is as American as apple pie. There are all kinds of things that you cannot privatize. Privatizing government will not work. You can't privatize a free and open public school system. Privatizing doesn't work on a federal level, it doesn't work on a state level, and it certainly won't work on a city level.

I pointed out that the corporations are buying the government. That means that the Democratic or Republican parties that used to hold government accountable have disappeared. There are no Democratic and Republican parties, except as money and advertising machines around election time. The parties now belong to the biggest celebrities and the corporations with the most dollars. Starting in 1994, Dick Morris and Bill Clinton ran an action on the American public with ads and focus groups for the 1996 presidential campaign. Today's Democratic Party is not the party of FDR or LBJ. The average American's politicalness is trained and developed by the received culture of television, image and sound replacing words. People don't even understand what "democratic society" means. Beyond images and sound bites, they're lost.

Let's take our school kids as an example. They're becoming illiterate. Robert Putman of Harvard points out that four hours in front of a television every day makes a passive body politic.[1] Teachers know that when children watch a couple of hours of television at night, it takes an hour and a half in the morning to get them out of passivity and into a mode where they can learn something. So they waste the first hour and a half because they're still passive from the images and the sounds that they slept with the night before. It's been documented. Adults are only grown children. We learn all our lives. We are not made complete. We grow when we're thirty, we grow when we're fifty, we grow when we're seventy. You cannot be bombarded with consumerism, debt, and constant worry about your job and security and have any energy left for the common good. You won't have three to five hours per week to have a public life.

So what happened that led to society's drawing off all of our energies into fighting for survival? It now takes two and a half incomes to support a family; sixty years ago it took one wage earner. It was called a "just wage." The programs of congregations take care of a lot of people today, not the federal government. Soup kitchens and the distribution of clothes and food are now handled primarily by local congregations. The left denigrates organized religion, and that is a big mistake. Where has the left disappeared to?

Civil society is structured on place, relationship, and tradition, not a ninety-day, bottom-line, nanosecond shifting around of money. The human person, the family, the congregation, and the volunteer organization are critical institutions. They are being systematically undermined by market forces abetted by the state's abdication of its proper role. This is the center of the American crisis. As British scholar Nicholas Boyle notes,

> . . . if globalization is the dominant world-historical process of the last century and a half, Americanization—first of America and then of the world—is the particular form in which it is realized. . . . The universal process of globalization has to become concrete in a particular form and it does so in the particular form of Americanization. Beyond individual statehood, for all of us, lies America.

The American Crisis, the unraveling of civil-society institutions that I've been describing here, is coming soon to a country near you.

Organizing Civil Society

The IAF is a national conversation about families, congregations, labor unions, and institutional power. It is about fundamental questions: Who will parent our children—teach, train, and nurture them? How will they be taught, trained, and nurtured? Will this formation take place in a strictly secular setting, where the system is said to be the solution, time is money, and profit is the sole standard of judgment? Or will the authentic teachers and prophets—parents and grandparents, pastors, rabbis, imams, and lay leaders—continue to convey the best values of the Jewish, Christian, Muslim, and other traditions to coming generations? Will workers have their say in the places where they labor and produce a next generation of organized workers? Can organized people hold organized money accountable in the new global marketplace?

The IAF doesn't organize congregations because of any high moral reasons, but because they are pockets of power with leadership and roots in local communities. These neighborhood institutions are the only ones that haven't been redlined. The fastest growing urban institutions are black Pentecostal and black Baptist churches. That's because people and families need a support system, and congregations, like unions, are natural support systems for families and community. People in congregations are available to be mobilized. Part of the IAF's deal is to get them out of the pews and into their communities. As a result of our success in doing that, we now have an interesting phenomenon going: After learning about a congregation's public life, some people who quit the church reconnect and come back. Others don't.

We organize people who have democratic values, not just church values. We hold relational meetings with as many unchurched as churched. Half of the people organizing out of a congregational base organize not only because of their faith values but also because of their democratic values. The labor movement isn't congregation-based, but it has thousands of local unions of organized people with values. These people are as committed to justice as anyone who goes to church. This is not an ideological issue for IAF. Ideology is utopian thinking; we operate in the world as it is with an eye toward the world as it could be. We also believe strongly that ordinary people, given the chance, will do the right thing. It's a basic, deep democratic belief that people are good, want good, and will stand for the whole if given the opportunity.

Our country is in the kind of crisis that both Madison and de Tocqueville warned us about. The intermediate voluntary institutions—including congregations and labor unions—are ineffectual in a power relationship with the powerful. As a result, the middle is collapsing, confused. The economic and political middle of this country is being sucked dry by a vacuum of power and meaning. The huge corporations, mass media, and "benevolent" government have moved into that vacuum. Those institutions in large part created the vacuum because the congregations and unions were not prepared for the new institutional arrangements and technologies that have overwhelmed us since World War II. We have given over control of much of our lives (including many tasks formerly exercised by families) to "experts" and "specialists," who are mostly fronts for institutions of greed and unaccountable power.

Without effective institutional power of their own, families, congregations, and labor unions withdraw, backbite, blame each other, or perhaps experiment with New Age fads—ignoring their history and strength. If families and congregations that are clear about their religious value base do not develop the capacity to negotiate institutionally, the masses of American families will continue to feel a decreasing sense of integration, centeredness, and confidence in their own relationship to other institutions. Families, congregations, and unions, as instruments of nurture, clarity, and protection for their members, will continue to lose their capacity to be effective.

We don't pretend to have the last word in this discussion, which is now going on among blacks, Hispanics, Asians, and whites in congregations, labor unions, and other local institutions in Boston and Chicago and Dallas, in Omaha and Phoenix, in San Antonio and East Los Angeles, in Baltimore and New Orleans, in New York and Portland. But we are clear on this: The clergy, women religious, lay leaders, congregation members, and labor leaders considering these questions in our organizations around the country are not interested in the three typical ways that people try to have a public life in America. They are not building a new movement or concerning themselves with construction of small civic organizations or simply trying to muscle in for a piece of civic clout. By way of background, I need to define these three approaches and describe the weaknesses of each.

Three Standard Approaches to Public Life

The first standard approach to public life is the charismatic movement. The movements of the 1960s and '70s—the civil rights movement, the antiwar movement, and the women's movement—were vivid, dramatic, and attractive. Each was built on an issue. Each was led by charismatic leaders. Each sought instant redress of grievances. "Peace Now." "Freedom Now." The tone was loose and rhetorical. Anyone could, and often did, jump into the demonstration or march. The structure was loose, too, and did not concentrate on training leaders. When the charismatic movement leaders were killed—Martin Luther King, Bobby Kennedy, Malcolm X, Tom Imboy, Chris Hasi, and Che Guevara—there was no large circle of well-developed leaders left to take up where they left off. The movement died with them. When the Chicago Seven were prosecuted by the federal government for conspiracy in Chicago, the government in effect froze their activity, internalized them in fund raising for their own defense, and strung them out in the courtroom for months. The glue of the movement was the romantic issue, the commitment to that issue, to the cause. When the cause collapsed, when the war ended, the movement collapsed with it. Is there a place for movement? Yes, but I'm not talking about that kind of mobilizing.

The dynamic of these movements tended to be sporadic. There were fits and starts, confused confrontations, strategies geared more to attract the attention of the media than to win. Members of these movements often concentrated on symbolic moral victories like placing flowers in the rifle barrels of National Guardsmen, embarrassing a politician for a moment or two, or enraging white racists. They often avoided any reflection about whether or not the moral victories led to any real change.

The money that supported these movements was outside money from wealthy liberal supporters, rather than hard money raised from participants. It could be withdrawn any time the establishment decided to do so.

Finally, the movements never attracted the moderate and conservative sections of the country. The majority of Americans considered members of these movements to be on the fringe, far away from the center of daily life, concerned with one issue or one value, willing to trample on traditions for the sake of a single cause.

The central weaknesses of all movements—reliance on charismatic leaders, failing to develop collective leadership, the lack of independence without a solid dues base, the tendency toward unfocused and unaccountable action, and the alienation of the moderates and conservatives—are all present today. The vivid images of the '60s and '70s continue to haunt us. Those struggles and images have created divisions in many parishes, congregations, synagogues, and mosques. On one side is a small band of social activists who continue to look for causes; on the other side is the overwhelming majority of moderates and conservatives who equate all social action with irresponsibility, confrontation for its own sake, and fanatical single-mindedness.

The second familiar approach to public life is the small civic organization. Most civic groups are forced to provide service to the residents of a defined turf, like a parish, a neighborhood, or a large apartment building. As in the movements, a civic group is a collection of individuals. The tone is often loose and light—friendly. The dynamic of most civic organizations is to react to crises. The smallness and parochialness of these organizations limits their ability to initiate, to head off crises, or to win larger victories. The scale of the organization limits the size of the targets the organization can address.

The style of these neighborhood-size structures tends to be schizophrenic: either overly procedural (mired in meetings and endless debates) or truly desperate (and thus always scrambling to react). The money that fuels these organizations is often other people's (foundation do-gooders), but the amounts tend to be small. In most communities, the local civic organization is on the fringe of the religious congregations in the area. While the congregations' social activists may be involved in the civic group, the majority of congregation members are glad to see someone involved but don't consider the group a central part of church life. In fact, these small civic groups sometimes are at odds with the central religious institutions of the community.

The third familiar approach to public life is the activity of the specialist in civic clout, the fixer, the insider: the neighbor whose brother works in city hall and can get a pothole in your street repaired; the local pol who rigs insurance exams so that his sons can pass; the pastor who asks for private favors from the alderman or city councilman that the ordinary citizen would never receive. This approach is what people cynically call politics as usual, the world where it's not what you know, it's who sent you.

When we talk about social action or building a serious citizens organization, a power organization, these three kinds of organizations tend to come to mind. We recall the clashes in Chicago during the 1968 Democratic convention or the pictures of dogs attacking citizens in Birmingham, monthly meetings of local business leaders over lunch, and the "best and brightest" cronyism that led the country into the Vietnam War.

These approaches do not suit the pressures, problems, and strains of the early twenty-first century. If the struggle for civil society is fought by the few remaining social action committees, or the new wave of VISTA volunteers, or those still waiting for the next charismatic leader, or if it is left to electoral politicians, it will surely be lost. Many of the reactions of the social activists produced Band-aid nonsolutions. Now, after nearly fifty years, it is clear that an analysis of who's got power and why, not of symptoms, is necessary if we are to relieve the stresses and heal the wounds.

Pressures on Civil Society

Who are the casualties of today's pressures on civil society? A Catholic pastor in McKeesport, Pennsylvania, talks about his own experience:

> The fears, frustration, and powerlessness of us all have become a way of life, as we constantly react to decisions made for us by others. I personally learned my values from my parents, from St. Vincent Seminary in Latrobe, Pennsylvania, and from the Catholic Church. I understand the importance and sacredness of life, self-respect, and dignity, both at home and in the church. However, neither family, church, nor seminary prepared me to fight for those same values or taught me how to translate those values into action against those who despise and reject them. I do not blame my family, my church, or the seminary for this; it is simply a statement of fact that these institutions of value were ill-equipped to teach me how to make my values a reality.

An iron worker in Pittsburgh tells of the refusal of his two sons to learn his craft from him. "So they had no trade, and when they came back from Vietnam, they couldn't get jobs," he recalled. "They went on welfare. Can you imagine, my sons on welfare? And finally welfare sent them for job training. You guessed it—welfare trained them in welding."

A Long Island executive explains, "We've got three kids in college now, in good schools. They cost us $25,000 apiece a year. It's killing us. It leaves nothing for retirement."

A Chicago working class mother wonders, "Who owns my kids? Us? Or all those professionals? I feel like my husband and I have to bargain for our kids with the school, the doctors, the talking heads on TV, the politicians. Pretty soon the kids are listening to them more than to us."

Another preacher says, "If you ask me what I look forward to, what I want most, what I need most, I'd tell you: money. I need money to run this monstrosity. I worry about money and administration and institutional politics, and I run like hell to keep pace with it all."

A minister in a suburban church asks, "Where are my people? Where are my leaders? I'm losing them—to television."

Finally, the principal of an inner-city parochial school recalls, "A gang selling narcotics across from the school was out there day and night in the coldest weather. Nothing stopped them. When the wind chill factor was forty-eight below they'd be there, with no hats or gloves, waiting for the cars to drive up. Then they'd pass them something and count their bills. I must have called the police at least forty times. I would call and identify myself and tell them what was going on. But nobody was following up on the information I was phoning into them. We felt the indifference to our problems by the police was an insult. Things were getting progressively worse. It is this kind of response that makes a neighborhood fall apart."

We know that the spinal cord of our society is the family. The family can be viewed organizationally as a small network of people, with a set of values and the ability to generate money through labor. The congregation is a network of families, with an explicit set of values, and with the ability to generate a substantial budget. The fundamental issue for the future is whether these institutions will survive the pressure being brought to bear against them. These pressures are threefold: economic, community, and cultural.

The modern American family has become a money machine. Month after month it must meet the bills for food, mortgage or rent, car and other transportation costs, insurance premiums, noninsured health items, clothing, taxes, utilities and fuel, school tuition and expenses, recreation, entertainment and travel, home maintenance, appliances, cosmetics and drugs, and contributions to charity. Congregations have similar burdens, plus staggering building maintenance costs, denominational assessments, and staff salaries to pay.

A second set of pressures comes from the immediate physical community. Almost every community is beginning to feel the accumulated corrosive effect of poverty, drug and alcohol abuse, and pornography. In Dallas, Los Angeles, Chicago, New York, and scores of other cities and towns, the air still stinks, and that stench wears at the health and morale of community residents. Crime doesn't respect the boundaries between city and suburb, suburb and town, town and country. Drug pushers are present in every major urban area from east to west. These conditions—some subtle, some obvious—combine to kill the human spirit. Watch frightened children walk down the middle of a street to avoid a group of toughs. Talk to members of a synagogue who are no longer involved in activities because they are afraid to leave their homes at night. Stand outside a door and listen to the long series of locks and latches that must be undone before you can enter a home. Talk to a Presbyterian pastor who has been robbed four times in eighteen months, robbed of more than his money, robbed of his vitality, his spirit. Listen to the landlord who wakes up to find graffiti scrawled across his neat two-flat with its freshly painted garage, his voice shaking with frustration and disgust.

The third set of pressures is cultural. Television is a profoundly parochial, addictive medium with an almost universal range. The networks transmit the simplistic stuff the advertisers want—basically money, luxury, sanitized sex, and the unaccountable violence of Hollywood—backed by billions in annual revenues. Television tells people how to eat, how to look, how to love, how to kill, and how to feel. It pumps out powerful images of what it is to be human, images frequently destructive of healthy family values. It devours space in family homes, where TVs in every room have become common, and devours time that families could spend together.

Another form of cultural pressure is the overscheduling that occurs in schools, in sports and community activities, and in congregations. Mothers become strung-out chauffeurs. Men and women who begin by wanting to help out at the church or the park get trapped into more and more work. Their free time is soon completely consumed.

The final form of cultural pressure is work, the expectation that work schedules are more important than family schedules, and the pressures that force those parents to work. In most families with school-age children, both parents must work to fuel the family money machine, to meet the basic costs of keeping the family going. Too often, children return from school to an empty home, or to parents so strapped by the demands of work, the tensions and frustrations of an environment seemingly out of their control, that they have little energy left for the love and care of the young ones.

These are the pressures that are draining the life out of civil society. If they continue to erode our relational and values base, the market and the state will lose the foundation on which they rest, and without which they can't survive.

Institutional Power

How do we begin to analyze the sources of those pressures on civil-society institutions? Where do the economic and cultural and community pressures originate? If we follow where our dollars go, we will find the institutions that shape our daily lives.

Our dollars end up in banks and savings and loans, in insurance companies, in oil companies, in utilities, and in the hands of major manufacturers, real estate developers, retailers, and organized criminals. These people speak with money. Banks, insurance companies, and organized crime provide capital for them. They buy the second level, the politicians, lawyers, the advertisers, the media. The media live on revenues from these institutions and rarely take the time to investigate and report the truth about the actual power relationships among these institutions. Unions are seldom prime decision-makers in a metropolitan area. Except in New York City, they are at best at the edge of major decisions. Lawyers and other professionals provide the rationales and jargon to perpetuate the top power institutions and screen them from the public.

Politicians get money, trips, and advance information from the money institutions. They are, however, in most cases only errand boys, or brokers at best. Chicago's late mayor, Richard M. Daley, was a classic broker between power institutions. He bossed the ward hacks and he brought the economic decision-makers (such as First National and Continental Banks) together to get their takeout from his development ideas. In New York, mayors have been errand boys for the economic institutions.

Lacking an accurate power analysis, most citizens' organizing efforts try to negotiate only with politicians and government bureaucracies. As a result, their energy is directed at the wrong rooms. They end up in "hearings" where they are "heard out" by "hearing officers" who are paid to hear but not make decisions. Smart politicians, professionals, and bureaucrats set up elaborate advisory hoops for citizens groups to jump through, effectively exhausting the citizens and taking them out of the arena. Meanwhile, the real decisions are sealed months before in elegant boardrooms.

One of the best examples of this process is found in Robert Caro's book on New York's Robert Moses, *The Power Broker*. The people of East Tremont, a working-class, mostly Jewish neighborhood in the Bronx, fought the needless destruction of their area by a leg of Moses' proposed Cross-Bronx Expressway. There were rallies, protests, petitions, hearings, and meetings with all levels of politicians. Robert Wagner, Jr., then a candidate for mayor, gave the citizens a clear, unequivocal promise that the expressway would not be built, that their area would not be destroyed. The group was aware of the power of Robert Moses, but they never dreamed that Moses could simply order Wagner to change his mind after he was elected. Moses did give the order; Wagner obeyed; East Tremont was destroyed. Not having made an accurate power analysis, the citizens group felt that the political apparatus, if pressured, would respond in good faith. Consequently, they had developed no leverage on the banks, contractors, the insurance companies, and the engineering and law firms that Moses had made rich. The mayor of the city of New York was a mere cog in the Moses power apparatus.

Decisions made by primary power institutions—institutions built upon the money of families and congregations—obviously have a major impact on the congregations and their families. When banks, insurance companies, and developers decide to build up a huge suburban area, congregational planners have to play catch-up with demographic trends. When financial institutions decide to redline city areas, those same planners and established congregations go through the agony of shutting down and merging congregations or subsidizing marginal operations. When major manufacturers decide to pull out of a community, thousands of church families are hurt badly by the sudden loss of jobs. When local economic establishments prevent industry from entering the area to avoid union organization, they destroy the hope for economic and social stability for thousands of families. When retailers abandon neighborhoods or buy into suburban shopping centers, family values, habits, and travel patterns are all affected along with the stability and future of the local congregations. When organized crime sells hard drugs in or near a school or introduces pornography and prostitution to a community or pulls the money of working people into sports betting and numbers, neighborhoods, congregations, and families suffer.

The point is not that all executives of all banks and corporations in America are bad people. Rather, the point is that the bottom-line value of these institutions, of "the system"—profit—is blind to the destruction of congregations and families. As long as they exhaust themselves with the middlemen, as long as families and congregations continue to struggle with politicians and the bureaucrats, the alignment of power will remain the same. The deterioration of family and congregational life will continue. The economic, community, and cultural pressures bearing down on them will increase to an intolerable point. The institutions that cause those pressures, mammoth machines lacking eyes, ears, and sensitivities, will continue, by instinct, to stamp society in their own images.

Developing a Politicalness for the Twenty-First Century

The traditional political parties will not work for the twenty-first century. The electoral machinery has been overgreased by corrupt corporate unilateral power—some call it market terrorism. Money, celebrity, and more money have gutted the authenticity of most political machines. FDR, Truman, and Eisenhower wouldn't recognize their political parties. What we now need are new institutional structures that attract moderates and idealists by giving them an instrument to use in channeling their energy to act as a counterbalance to the state and the market.

This century's refounders must create new instruments for public life based not on technology or science but on communal habits of the heart. New radical, nonpartisan, international assemblies must be created and fostered as countervailing institutions. By providing average citizens with a means of group action through which they can participate actively in the public democratic process, the new organizations that we need will offer a more public and personal source for political participation than the media, focus groups, and attitude and opinion polls. Much of this civic work is presently being done, but on too small a scale and size and not across national boundaries. I hope the European Union may help lead the way.

The old public life instruments—the neighborhood, the city council, the town meeting—are obsolete. Their scale is wrong for the twenty-first century. Labor unions are a good example of organizing on the right scale, but they also are under attack by union-busting corporations and firms. The largest voluntary, civil-society organizations are still religious organizations with a large number of loyal and generous people involved in institutional mainte-nance, while neglecting public justice issues. We need new kinds of voluntary associations to find new ways to participate in complex urban life, ways that will create social power, new energy, and opportunities to pursue enlightened self-interest.

In the real world as it is, there are no global, national, or state problems or solutions. Will-o'-the-wisp, large-scale solutions to problems like "pov-erty" keep us from engaging the local public issues that we have the power to do something about. That's why ideologues, liberals, and do-gooders rarely produce. They talk, gossip, complain, and hang on to their obsolete theories. Most of them would screw up a two-car funeral. Particularity is the test of any theory, ideology or "ism." IAF leaders and organizers are specific and particular. They have budgets, personnel, and a mission. They exist. They do large and small collective action and reflection hourly, daily, and even on weekends. William Greider captures the heart of these organizations well:

> The quality that makes the IAF organizations so distinctive is their relent-less attention to the conditions that ordinary people describe in their own lives. Their authority is derived from personal experience, not from the policy experts of formal politics. . . . IAF gives up short-term celebrity on "hot issues" in order to develop the long-term power of a collective action that is real.[2]

IAF organizations are in place and position to initiate and act; we just need more of them. They are pragmatic and realistic about the human condition. They know that every positive has a negative, and vice versa. A multi-issued, broad-based slant protects them against isolation, against being too small, too task-oriented, or controlled by one or two people. They seek out other organizations for support and a mix of strengths. They never buy their own propaganda.

IAF organizations also do not believe in the traditional left/right doxology. A much more insightful approach is needed for politics. The great masses of people are neither to the left or the right. They are moderates, and which way they lean on any given issue depends. People aren't naturally ideological; that's an acquired brainwash. The IAF's commitment to stay with and build on the moderate middle is why we insist that you don't only organize those who look, think, or pray like you or share your neighborhood or tax bracket. Social and political diversity must be seen as strength. People have more in common and through shared experiences will cooperate. For examples, take a look at the United States and the European Union today. Very soon, one-half of the world's population will be living in major metropolitan cities of the world. That's one reason that we need less abstract theory and more thought on how immigrants are going to fit into urban metropolises.

Unless participation and involvement are restored to the center of a controlled capitalism, unless the market is kept in its place by large, powerful organizations whose members are civil-society institutions, the twenty-first century will bring increased alienation and frustration to its citizens. Human beings are political animals. Our muscles must be exercised or they atrophy. Our politicalness is our sovereignty, our self-governance. Nations aren't sovereign, the human person is. Public life is for all. Large numbers of everyday, ordinary leaders must commit one, three, or ten hours a week, every week, to pursue the common good through right relationships. Let's be realistic. You don't need everybody. A well organized 3 to 5 percent is enough to start serious social change. Not any 3 to 5 percent, but key people and institutions that others follow.

To be effective, this work must be done in collectives with others. Sharing concerns through relational meetings, house meetings, assemblies, and councils for deliberation must happen. The size and scale must be appropriate to the new century, and that means metropolitan or regional, city, suburban and rural communities together; upstate and downstate clusters; statewide and regional strategic plans and actions. The accountability of elected officials to organized people instead of to organized money is at the heart of all this. The inclusion of all people in pluralistic configurations of informed and engaged citizens is the great task facing our century. Jefferson urged a revolution every twenty-five years. Our most recent revolutions were the birth-control pill, nuclear power, the Internet, and unbridled consumerism. Aren't we about due for another?

Politics is an activity. It's not a thing. It's not the implementation of abstract principles. It cannot be held. It is always given and received. Politics and love are the only forms of constraint possible between free people. As Bill Greider says in the passage I quoted in the first pages of this book,

> Politics is not a game. It exists to resolve the largest questions of the society—the agreed-upon terms by which everyone can live peaceably

with one another. At its best politics creates and sustains social relationships—the human conversation and engagement that draw people together and allow them to discover their mutuality.[3]

Public life is a means to moral meaning, but that meaning cannot be realized by individuals acting in isolation, or acting only with their own kind. Developing politicalness in the twenty-first century means learning to act powerfully and effectively in public with others who are different, and that includes people from other countries.

Radical, Nonpartisan Assemblies

This century's founders and refounders must create new political instruments not based on science and technology, but rather on culture, on what de Tocqueville called "habits of the heart" in the book he wrote on American democracy more than 150 years ago. New mediating organizations must be created and fostered. Some of the energy now being poured into capitalism ought to be redirected into global civil society to strengthen small organizations like family, congregation, labor unions, and civic groups—small, sustainable communities within large urban areas.

I'm not calling for replacing or destroying structures controlled by money, but something like the following. Most people pour huge amounts of money into personal life; we are made that way. We expend large amounts of energy at our jobs, to sustain our families and sometimes because work is meaningful. What we need in addition to private economic and vocational choices are institutional structures invented by moderates and idealists across the globe who want something more than work and consumption as a way of life. The vocation of inventing these structures is to have a meaningful public life. Much of this work in civil society is being done, but on too small a size and scale.

Radical, nonpartisan assemblies crossing national boundaries are the sane alternative to the so-called war on terrorism, which relies on violence and death, and which will fail in our global society. The last century should have taught us that violence only begets more violence. We need less talk about missile shields and more about how immigrants from thirty-five to forty different countries are going to be integrated into the urban centers of the world. What I'm lifting up here is a new approach for the one world descending on us. "Empire U.S.A." with its "axis of evil" sound bites will fail. The men, women, and young people of this century must let go of the illusion of rugged individualism and embrace a relational construct, making connections across differences of nation, culture, and class. That can only begin locally, through the calculated organization of moderates and flexible conservatives and liberals. Ideologists hate a real relational culture. Utopians are always looking for a shortcut to nirvana. The extremists and antis will be against this, but together they represent only a small percentage of people. Totalitarian types will try to destroy such efforts. But apathy is the worst enemy of relational culture.

If people, especially young people, see some daylight, some new opportunities and different challenges, change can take place. I'm arguing for a serious national and international effort. Its funding must be independent—dues-based—with no government funds for its operating budget. People will support an effort that's authentic, nonpartisan, and grounded in good professional organizing. I'm moving on, but there is a network of trained nonpartisan organizers in the U.S., Britain, Germany, South Africa, and beginning in Central America who can be foundational to this approach. Lack of imagination is our only stumbling block.

Just as we pour all kinds of energy into birthing, nurturing, and educating our next generation and into our careers, why can't we pour energy into public-life ventures, into assemblies that are multi-issue, freely chosen, and built to create a more free and open society? Why don't we build more social capital to counterbalance unbridled financial capital? The European Union is one example of an effort to organize as more than an economic unit. The U.S. government–funded Peace Corps was a weak attempt in this direction.

I'm talking about something radical here, systematic and ongoing organizing for collective fairness, justice, and equality—all the habits of the heart required for what we frequently call the common good. We have professionals for this and professionals for that—why not thousands of professionally trained organizers paid by the people they work for to create these new political instruments in our global world?

Appendix

Industrial Areas Foundation Network

IAF Trustees

Marvin D. Wurth, President; D. Barry Menuez, Vice President; Jean Bethke Elshtain, Secretary; Thomas Boodell Jr., Treasurer; Talat Othman, Hays H. Rockwell, Bishop John Adams, Rev. Johnny Ray Youngblood, and Edward Chambers

IAF National Organizers

Edward Chambers—Executive Director

Executive Team

Arnold Graf, Ernesto Cortes Jr., Michael Gecan, Christine Stephens, and Margaret McKenzie

National Staff: Gerald Taylor, Pearl Ceasar, Stephen Roberson, Maribeth Larkin, Jonathan Lange, and Frank Pierson

ABLE
542 Moreland Avenue SE
Atlanta, GA 30316
(404) 627–8284

Action in Montgomery
13925 New Hampshire Avenue
Silver Spring, MD 20904
(301) 388–0700

Albuquerque Interfaith
6001 Marble Avenue NE, Suite 11
Albuquerque, NM 87110
(505) 268–3991

Allied Communities of Tarrant (ACT)
P. O. Box 3565

Fort Worth, TX 76113
(817) 332–1830

The AMOS Network (Mississippi)
350 West Woodrow Wilson, Suite 3230
Jackson, MS 39213
(601) 364–1091

Arizona Interfaith Network
1802 E. Thomas Road, Suite #15
Phoenix, AZ 85016

Austin Interfatih
1301 South IH35, #313
Austin, TX 78741
(512) 916–0100

Baltimoreans United for Leadership Development (BUILD)
2114 North Charles Street
Baltimore, MD 21218
(410) 528–0305

Baltimore County Sponsoring Committee
9019 Liberty Road
Randallstown, MD 21133

Bay Area Organizing Committee
4319 Geary Boulevard
San Francisco, CA 94118
(415) 751–6174

Berlin, Germany Sponsors
Schoneweide, Neukolln, Hamburg
Nebringster 17
D14059
Berlin, Germany
(011) 49 30326 08435

The Border Organization
P. O. Box 806
Eagle Pass, TX 78853
(830) 773–2590

Central Coast Interfaith Sponsors
95 Alta Vista Avenue
Watsonville, CA 95076
(831) 728–3210

Citizens Organizing Foundation (COF)
112 Cavell Street
London, E1 2JA
England
(011) 44 207 375 1658

COPS/Metro
925 San Pedro
San Antonio, TX 78212
(210) 222–8562

Corpus Christi Area Church of the Reconciliation
4518 Saratoga Blvd.
Corpus Christi, TX 78413
(361) 852-9677

Dallas Area Interfaith
1104 Lupo Drive
Dallas, TX 75207
(214) 689–5988

Dane County Sponsors
3614 Alpine Road
Madison, WI 53704
(608) 334-5890

Des Moines (Amos)
3700 Cottage Grove
Des Moines, IA 50311
(515) 255-5400

DuPage United
515 Wheaton Avenue
Wheaton, IL 60187
(630) 327–8775

Durham Metropolitan
201 S. Alston Ave.
Durham, NC 27701
(919) 530–8515

East Brooklyn Congregation (EBC)
440 Watkins Avenue
Brooklyn, NY 11212
(718) 498–4099

East Valley Interfaith Sponsoring Committee
c/o Dayspring United Methodist Church
1365 East Elliot Road
Tempe, AZ 85284
(602) 831–6918

El Paso Interreligious Sponsoring Committee (EPISO)
7134 Alameda
El Paso, TX 79915
(915) 778–3200

Greater Boston Interfaith Organization
307 Bowdoin Street
Boston, MA 02122
(617) 825–5600

Greater Edmonton Alliance
Edmonton, Canada
(503) 235-6233

Helping Empower Local People (HELP)
P.O. Box 34008
Charlotte, NC 28234
(704) 372–5812

**Houston Area Organization/Fort Bend
   Interfaith**
3400 Montrose, Suite 907
Houston, TX 77006
(713) 807–1429

IAF (Texas)
1106 Clayton Lane, Suite 120W
Austin, TX 78723

The Jeremiah Group
P.O. Box 2674
Marrero, LA 70072
(504) 522-3493

Justice Alliance Education Fund
(Eastern Washington Action and Justice
   Alliance)
1526 East 11th
Spokane, WA 99202
(509) 532–1688

Lake County United
P.O. Box 726
29700 N. St. Mary's Road
Libertyville, IL 60048
(847) 266–9803

**Long Island CAN (Congregations,
   Associations, and Neighborhoods)**
45 Everette Street
Valley Stream, NY 11580
(516) 733–4590

Los Angeles Metropolitan Sponsors
1545 Wilshire Boulevard, Suite 328
Los Angeles, CA 90017
(213) 273–8420

Lower Manhattan Together
173 East Third Street
New York, NY 10009
(212) 673–9463

Northern Louisiana Interfaith
P. O. Box 7553
Monroe, LA 71211
(318) 324–9706

**Omaha Together One Community
   (OTOC)**
3035 Harney Street
Suite 100
Omaha, NE 68131
(402) 344–4401

The Organizing Project
1244 Northeast 39th Avenue
Portland, OR 97232
(503) 235–6233

Philadelphia Interfaith Action (PIA)
4950-B Rising Sun Ave.
Philadelphia, PA 19120
(215) 329–8804

Pima County Interfaith Council (PCIC)
78 West Cushing Street
Tucson, AZ 85701
(520) 903–2333

Puget Sound Vision
9421 18th Avenue SW
Suite 202
Seattle, WA 98106
(206) 762–9830

Queens Citizens Organization
85–18 61st Road
Rego Park, NY 11374
(718) 898–4194

Rural Nebraska
c/o Interchurch Ministries of Nebraska
215 Centennial Mall South, Suite 411
Lincoln, NE 68508

**Sacramento Valley Organizing
Community**
3263 1st Avenue
Sacramento, CA 95817
(916) 457–0245

South Bronx Churches (SBC)
389 East 150th Street
Bronx, NY 10455
(718) 665–5564

Triangle Interfaith Project
808 B North Memorial Parkway, Suite 104B
Nederland, TX 77627
(409) 722–5565

Tying Nashville Together (TNT)
P. O. Box 121371
Nashville, TN 37212
(615) 327–2625

United Power for Action & Justice
P.O. Box 11865
Chicago, IL 60611
(312) 245–9211

Upper Manhattan Together
125 East 105th Street
New York, NY 10029
(212) 369–4106

The Valley Interfaith Project
1802 East Thomas Road
Suite #15
Phoenix, AZ 85016
(602) 248–0607

Valley Interfaith
114 North Texas Street
Mercedes, TX 78570
(956) 565–6316

Washington D.C. Interfaith Network
c/o Luther Place Memorial Church
1226 Vermont Avenue NW
Washington, DC 20005
(202) 518–0815

West Texas Organizing Project
P.O. Box 5237
Lubbock, TX 79408–5237
(806) 793–1467

**Yuma County Interfaith Sponsoring
Committee**
Immaculate Conception Catholic Church
505 Avenue B
Yuma, Arizona 85364

Main contact for IAF network affiliates:

Industrial Areas Foundation
220 West Kinzie Street, Fifth Floor
Chicago, IL 60610
(312) 245–9211

Notes

Introduction: The Industrial Areas Foundation—
Social Knowledge, Power, and Politicalness

1. Saul Alinsky, *Reveille for Radicals* (New York: Vintage, 1946) and *Rules for Radicals* (New York: Vintage, 1971).
2. William Greider, *Who Will Tell the People* (New York: Simon & Schuster, 1992), pp. 13–14.
3. Sheldon Wolin, *The Presence of the Past* (Baltimore: Johns Hopkins University Press, 1989), p. 139.

Chapter 1: The World As It Is and the World As It Should Be

1. Hannah Arendt, *The Human Condition* (Chicago: University of Chicago Press, 1958), pp. 7–8.
2. Bernard Loomer, "Two Kinds of Power," in Bernard Lee, *The Future Church of 140 B.C.E.* (New York: Crossroad, 1995), pp. 169–202.
3. Nicolai Berdyaev, *The Destiny of Man,* translated by Natalie Duddington and Geoffrey Bles (New York: Harper & Row, 1937), p. 56.
4. Johann B. Metz, quoted in *Cultural-Political Interventions in the Unfinished Project of Enlightenment,* ed. Thomas McCarthy (Cambridge, Mass.: MIT Press, 1992), p. 181.

Chapter 3: Broad-Based Organizing:
An Intentional Response to the Human Condition

1. Arendt, *The Human Condition,* chap. 5.
2. Henri Bergson, *Creative Evolution,* translated by Arthur Mitchel (London: Macmillan) p. 186.

3. Bernard McClaverty, *Grace Notes* (New York: W. W. Norton, 1998).

4. Arendt, *The Human Condition,* p. 177.

5. Ibid., p. 178.

6. Ibid., p. 8.

7. Karl Marx, *Capital,* vol. 1, translated by Samuel Moore and Edward Aveling (New York: International Publishers, 1967), pp. 146–55.

8. Wolin, *The Presence of the Past,* p. 139.

9. Abraham Heschel, *The Prophets,* vol. 1 (New York: Harper & Row, 1962), p. 16.

10. Bernard Crick, *In Defence of Politics,* 2nd edition (Chicago: University of Chicago Press, 1972), pp. 25–26.

11. Max Weber, "Politics as a Vocation," in *From Max Weber: Essays in Sociology,* translated and edited by Hans H. Gerth and C. Wright Mills (New York: Oxford University Press, 1958), p. 128.

Chapter 5: The Practice of Public Life:
Research, Action, and Evaluation

1. Alinsky, "Tactics," *Rules for Radicals,* pp. 126–64.

Chapter 8: Thoughts on Twenty-First-Century Challenges

1. Robert Putnam, *Bowling Alone* (New York: Simon & Schuster, 2000), pp. 221–24.

2. Greider, *Who Will Tell the People,* p. 234.

3. Ibid., pp. 13–14.

Index